C000085727

Odd Man Out in the Alps

Published by
Stacey International
128 Kensington Church Street
London W8 4BH
Tel: +44 (0)20 7221 7166 Fax: +44 (0)20 7792 9288
E-mail: info@stacey-international.co.uk
www.stacey-international.co.uk

© Sir Ron Norman 2008

ISBN: 978-1905299-88-1

Designed by
Kitty Carruthers

Cover illustration by
Natacha Ledwidge

Illustrated by
Peter Bew

Printed in the UAE

All rights reserved. No part of this publication may be reproduced
or transmitted in any form or by any means without the permission
of the copyright owners.

British Library Catalogue in Publication Data:
A catalogue record for this book is available from
the British Library.

Odd Man Out
in the
Alps

Sir Ron Norman

STACEY
INTERNATIONAL

Acknowledgements

The drawings in this book are the work of my good friend Peter Bew. Sophia Bartleet reminded me of the basic principles of English grammar. Kitty Carruthers edited the work with great skill, often having to remind me not to use two words where one would do (the job perfectly well).

When you write a book you learn who your friends are. Friends get subjected to readings on long car journeys or are expected to read great tracts overnight. They tread on egg-shells; are they simply expected to congratulate and smarm or are they required to make constructive criticism? Difficult questions with different answers on different days.

My friends have come through these tests with flying colours and I thank them: Sheila Darling, John and Ann Gatenby, John Lund and Alice Thwaite.

My marriage has survived the tribulations of writing a book, just as it has survived many a trial over the years. I love my wife Jo.

RN

Contents

Chapter One

Time for Plan D

It was a sunny morning in late August. I was sitting on the sun deck of the steamer ferrying me along Lake Geneva, in pole position in the front deck chair, with unimpeded views to left, right and centre. My gaze took in the wooded shoreline, followed the patchwork of green and brown hills and rose to the snow-capped mountains on the horizon. Away to the south, I could just make out Mont Blanc glittering in the sun, demure and gentle, her glaciers and snow-clad slopes a seductive, rosy-white outline in a distant purple haze. The mountains beckoned and I could hardly wait to get among them. I curbed my impatience by concentrating on the attractions closer to hand.

The ferry chugged back and forth across the lake, docking at postcard-pretty villages. As we zig-zagged between the French and Swiss banks, I caught sight of grand old houses, mostly built in the local stone, their delicate cream colour contrasting with occasional patches of pinkish render, and brief, tantalizing glimpses of courtyards, of churches and of gardens. I bobbed from one side of the boat to the other like an over-excited schoolboy on his first outing. There were scenes all around begging to be photographed – but my camera did not work. The battery was flat and I had forgotten to bring the charger.

This was the start of what I had originally intended as the most meticulously organized expedition of all time. My plan was to walk four hundred miles along that great footpath, the Grand Randonée Cinq (GR5) from Lake Geneva to Nice. But so far, that was the full extent of my plan. I had no idea how long I would take, no idea where or when I might stop each day. It would all depend on the scenery, the weather, the wine or whatever. I would simply take things as I found them.

As I had told anyone who would listen, to walk through the French Alps for two weeks carrying everything I needed on my back required the detailed planning of a military operation. Weeks before the off, I laid out every item I would need in the spare room. I held heated debates with myself – should I take four pairs of socks or three? Should I or should I not take a washing-line and clothes pegs? I consulted learned medical opinion as to whether I really needed pills that opened my bowels when I was already carrying pills that closed them. I checked, weighed and re-checked every item. I cut my bar of soap in half to save weight. My rucksack was packed and re-packed until there was a place for everything and everything was in its place.

Except for the battery charger. So much for all that careful planning. It did not inspire confidence in a successful expedition.

I remembered two spectacular occasions when my camera had failed me. My wife and I were once in a tiny plane being flown up the Grand Canyon, a hair-raising flight around the pinnacles and beneath the rim. My camera jammed just before take-off so I have no record of that momentous flight with which to impress my friends. But the images are seared on my brain; panoramic, technicolour pictures of incredible rock formations and breathtaking scenery.

On the other occasion, we were in India perched on the back of an elephant. I was staring into the glittering eye of a displeased tigress, not ten feet away, and I ran out of film. There is more menace per millimetre in a tiger's eye than in any other beast in the animal kingdom. I will never forget the look as she began to lose her temper, particularly when she was close enough to touch, and even more particularly when there were no bars between us, nothing to protect us – unless you count the elephant.

Neither aerial photographs of the Grand Canyon, nor spine-chilling close-ups of tigers decorate my walls. On the other hand, my memories of both events are all the more vivid since I was gripped by the excitement of the moment, not fussing over shutter speeds and separated by a lens.

Heartened by these reflections, I recognized that the omens for this trip could be favourable after all. But the situation demanded a new plan. I had bought a ticket for the boat journey all the way along the lake to the last French village of St Gingolph, where I was looking forward to spending a relaxing evening. The question was, would I find a camera shop in such a small place? Playing safe, I went ashore at Evian-les-Bains. The town is famous throughout Europe for its mineral water – surely it was big enough to sell cameras. More by luck than judgement, I stumbled upon a shop selling photographic equipment. The owner told me with great emphasis that there was not in the entire Republic of France either a battery or a charger to fit my particular camera. But Monsieur could supply a very similar camera at an exceptionally modest price. I reviewed the strength of my negotiating position and surrendered unconditionally. I bought the new camera and caught a taxi to St Gingolph.

Thoroughly irritated with myself for my forgetfulness, I was no longer in the right frame of mind for a relaxing evening, and decided that I would start walking that day.

The Swiss-French border cleaves St Gingolph clean in two. Armed customs officers in dull grey uniforms man the concrete booths, and border guards, in drab khaki and bristling with weapons, control the steel gates. The atmosphere was dark, forbidding, threatening. It brought back chilling memories of National Service, the Iron Curtain, clicking heels and hostility. The hairs on the back of my neck tingled.

A sweet black coffee at a lakeside restaurant brought me back to more cheerful reality. By 2 o'clock, I was off. Plan C would now swing smoothly into operation; I would walk for two hours and stay the night at a comfortable hotel in the small village of Novel. My taxi-driver, an unsmiling ramrod of a woman, obviously ex-military, had been proud to inform me as she stiffened to attention that this was the birthplace of Francois Mitterrand, one-time President of France.

The ex-military in *me* rose to the challenge. I marched off through the town, shoulders back, stomach in, walking tall. Southwards, onwards and upwards, Mont Blanc here I come. I wheeled to the left, marched under the railway bridge, strode up the hill – and was lost. Not the start my old CO would have expected. I asked for directions back to the GR5 for the first, but certainly not for the last, time. Apparently I should first have taken a right and gone under a different bridge; then it was over the hill, round the bend and Nice was straight ahead.

At last, I was on the right path, with enthusiasm and excitement propelling me forward as if I had rockets on my heels. Civilisation soon gave way to dense and ancient woodlands of beech, oak and ash, and some fir. The track follows the valley of the Morge River, the boundary between France and Switzerland at this point. It is a placid stream in summer, but piles of splintered tree-trunks littered the valley floor, suggesting a furious torrent in the winter. The track zigs and zags up the steep slope, careful never to present too severe a gradient. Many of these hill tracks are hundreds of years old. Ancient man, without the benefit of spirit-level or theodolite but with generations of accumulated wisdom, found the best routes to get laden packhorses up the hillsides.

Fourteen stone is a lot of body to get up a hill. It was hot and windless and humid under the canopy of trees. Soon salty sweat was trickling down my face and into my eyes. I needed one hand to wipe my eyes, and the other to flick away the flies. My pack felt twice as heavy as it had on my practice walks. The combination of the sweat, the flies and the weight made me realise what life must be like for a packhorse. 'Things can only get better,' I repeated like a mantra to my cynical alter ego.

When it comes to walking, I am the odd man out. I always walk in sandals. Proper walkers, booted and gaitered, with walking poles and Lucozade drip-fed into their mouths, look at me with a mixture of condescension and pity.

'Doesn't this idiot know that you have to spend big bucks on equipment before you can go walking?'

Then the questions start. 'Surely your feet get wet?'

'No, I am wearing waterproof socks.'

'You must slip a lot?'

'Not at all, I am as surefooted as a goat.'

'Surely you'll twist your ankle?'

'Maybe, but so far I have walked about a thousand miles without a problem.'

In fact, I have lost count of the expensively-equipped walkers I have overtaken as they hobbled along with blisters, bruised toes or cramp. I prefer to carry minimal kit, to wear sandals and walk without a care in the world.

Much to my surprise, the first stretch was not as gruelling as I had expected and I arrived at Novel by mid-afternoon. Walking out of the woods at Novel was like poking my head out of my sleeping bag at daybreak, dark shadows transformed into bright expectations. All around me was a kaleidoscope of mountain views. The panorama swept from the distinctive fang of the Dent d'Oche in the west, round to the high cliffs of the Swiss Gramont in the east. I am exhilarated every time I move into the mountains; my throat goes dry and I get butterflies in my stomach from sheer excitement. Knowing that this landscape was a mere foretaste of the pleasures ahead added to my euphoria and I skipped along the path like a little kid. The sun came out and the clouds rolled back. I was striding out beneath a sky so blue that I thought I must have strayed into a holiday commercial. The sunlight, low-angled and warmly yellow by this time of day, picked out every verdant shade across the hillside, from the bottle-green of the conifer stands to the palest yellow-green of the saxifrages. The day was only half over, the adrenalin was flowing and I was in the mood. It was time for Plan D. When I reached the village I asked a group of people, in my inadequate French, if there was any accommodation within a three hour walk. They were friendly and all spoke at once in their eagerness to help me

'*D'accord,*' said they, followed by a cascade of French which I took to mean, 'There are chalets at Neuteu, three hours away, and there you will get a bed but no food.'

On the off-chance that I might find some food to take with me, I called at the hotel. There was another walker in the garden, having a beer. Two beers later, I knew that Stephen was a computer programmer from Hackney; a cockney who lived happily enough in spite of his lack of aspirates. He told me that 'e 'ad read about the GR5 and, looking for a free-and-easy 'oliday, 'ad decided to 'ave a go!' He did not have the build of a walker. Short, stumpy and muscular, he had the physique more of a Westmoreland wrestler than a Cumbrian fell-runner. Wisely, he had decided to acclimatise himself gently, and after leaving St Gingolph that morning, was spending the afternoon recuperating and giving his system a chance to get used to the local beer.

He told me, 'It's OK, this GR5, but there's too much effing upping!'

With a French loaf poking out of my pack and some cheese in my pocket, I set off for the Chalets Neuteu. I quickly realised that Stephen was in for an unpleasant surprise when his analytic brain took in how quickly the easy foothills became hard mountains. The dark woodlands gave way to shimmering grassland, with clumps of trees dotted around, rather like the grounds of a stately home. Between the stands, breathtaking views of far horizons claimed my attention in all directions. The friendly, well-graded tracks fade away after Novel and the going gets tougher. This is no well-designed packhorse trail now; this is a route selected, with obvious malice aforethought, by capricious and extremely agile goats. Stony tracks lead directly up steep slopes; so steep in places that I had to scramble up on hands and knees. My brain resented every gram I was carrying and scrolled through a mental check-list searching for any item to discard. Surely, I could manage without a toothbrush? Only a fop needs a comb. In this frame of mind, people who carry two litres of water appear to me to be lunatics. Two litres weighs five pounds, for heaven's sake! The medics tell me that it is essential to drink two litres of water a day, but, unless I am on a route-march across the Kalahari Desert, why should I carry every drop of it with me? I carry a half-litre bottle of water and a few purification tablets. Not only do I save nearly four pounds of weight, but I'm awash with smug superiority.

Two hours out of Novel, I was forcing my aching and rebellious body up the last hill towards the Chalets Neuteu when I heard voices. Who should be there to greet me, but my friends from the village? So inadequate is my French that I had not picked up from the conversation that they owned the chalets and were heading there themselves. They had stocked up with food and wine and gone ahead using four-wheel drive vehicles and private forest tracks. Now they tell me!

Jean-Marie and his wife Amelia, I soon discovered, were holidaying with their own children as well as a swarm of nephews, nieces and second cousins, and Grandma too. They were a family of boundless generosity and bouncing exuberance. To them, everything was a laugh and nothing was a problem. Even with a 4x4, they had to walk a considerable distance and climb a steep and rocky path to reach the chalets. Just below us, with the aid of a walking-stick, a few paces at a time, came eighty-five-year-old Great Grandma. She had always come on holiday with her great-grandchildren; why should this year be different? She made it to the chalets and got a standing ovation from her family. If only I had had a yellow jersey to present – nobody deserved a prize for gutsy determination more than she.

Despite the altitude, I was hot and sticky. I stripped off to enjoy a wash in the communal water-butt, challengingly placed in the middle of the circle formed by the three huts. The ice-cold, mountain water gushes freely by the giga-gallon into this public bath and yet surely it could not be very different from the water that is bottled and sold for an exorbitant price just over the hill at Evian-les-Bains? These water-butts are distinctive; a stylish yet practical feature of the farms and villages of this part of the French Alps. I am all in favour of any design where the form flows from the function, as these did, quite literally. The butt itself is a tree trunk about a metre in diameter and perhaps three metres long, laid on its side, with a big rectangular basin hacked out of its full length. A hollowed-out swan-necked branch stands vertically over the basin like a mammoth mixer-tap over a bath. The water comes snaking down a pipe from high up the mountain and up through the swan-neck, finally cascading out into the basin, bubbling, splashing and gurgling an inviting melody of water music. My strip-wash was alternately torturous and exhilarating. Mountain water is only freezing cold for the first thirty seconds; after that, the nervous system blows a fuse and fails to register any feeling at all. Lying outstretched on the grass in the warm, late afternoon sun was a great way to allow the nervous system to recover – and to get my washing dried.

The Chalets Neuteu sit just below the eastern end of the peak of the Dent d'Oche, that giant sentinel of the Alps I had seen from the ferry only this morning. On the last shoulder of the Dent d'Oche ridge, just above Neuteu, stands a small shrine. A stone pillar has been set on a circle of steps to support a stone box with a metal-grilled door. Through the grille, I could see the painted statue of a saint standing serenely and decorated with a few, faded dried flowers. The whole structure is about seven feet high, and is all the more impressive for its unexpectedness. It must date from the time when Neuteu was a sheiling, the upper pasture where shepherds brought their flocks for summer grazing. The paddocks and cottages have long-since fallen derelict, except for those few now restored as chalets. It struck me forcibly that faith had outlived the stone-built cottages. Somebody, over the decades of dereliction, had cared for and respected this remote shrine.

When I showed interest, Jean-Marie told me that the shrine was dedicated to St Roch. Two teenage girls, giggling, stuttering and stumbling with their English, yet totally unimpressed by my ha'p'orth of French, attempted to persuade me to adopt St Roch as my guiding saint. 'St Roch, 'e is a special man for the *pelerin*. 'E is very good for you.' Since the Middle Ages, he has been popular with pilgrims and travellers; there are many chapels and shrines to him that have survived along the ancient pilgrim routes of Europe. His popularity stems from his reputation for healing travellers' sicknesses and, particularly, in seeing off the plague. Almost converted, I thought that perhaps I could do without those two sets of pills if I walked under the benevolent gaze of St Roch? To hedge my bets, I bowed to St Roch but kept the pills.

Jean-Marie and I sat on the steps at the base of the shrine looking north over the six miles and the five thousand feet that I had covered that afternoon from Lake Geneva. The lake itself was still just visible, dark, purple and brooding in the evening light but cheered by the faint, sparkling diamante of lights of Lausanne on the far distant shore. We sat in silent appreciation of the scene. Jean-Marie breathed easy-going conviviality to his family and visitor alike. We had very few words in common, certainly not enough for a philosophical debate on the meaning of life, yet we sat in companionable silence over a bottle of Apremont Masson, a local wine that might have made some small contribution to the magic of the evening.

I may have travelled only a few miles but I had come a very long way from the bustle of modern city life to the timeless tranquility of the mountains. The day had started at an airport hotel with an elegant breakfast served on those white, curvy-sided Villeroy and Bosch plates I like so much. It was finishing with a plain supper of bread and cheese on a chipped enamel plate that would not raise a starting-bid on e-Bay. At the start, I had paid good money for bottled water. At the finish, I had an abundance of free, fresh, sparkling mountain water. Which of these starkly different worlds did I prefer? On those steps, in that tranquility, there was only one answer. The real question was, would the mood last all the way to the Mediterranean?

In that setting I was reminded of my very first mountain climb. I climbed Ben Nevis on my fiftieth birthday to prove to myself that I was not *that* old, and because I wanted to lay to rest the slight unease I'd always felt about high mountains. Although it was early May, a blizzard was blowing. In a white-out, I managed to navigate my way with a compass to the small summit hut. My Boy Scout training had, at last, paid dividends. There were two young men in the hut, one adequately kitted out and cheerful, the other dressed for a summer stroll on the South Downs and unconscious with hypothermia. The two of us carried the dead weight of that idiot through the snow to below the blizzard line. There, with the impertinence of youth, he quickly recovered and they wandered off down the mountain. I was in a state of near exhaustion, literally brought to my knees by the physical effort. The incident gave me confidence and wiped away my unease with mountains, though I have never quite understood why it planted in me the bug to climb every mountain that I could find. But it did and I have been climbing or trekking in mountains all over the world for the twenty years since.

As the sun went down, we saw shadows moving slowly along the hillside, about half a mile away, on the other side of the valley. Amelia and Jean-Marie identified a trio of moufflon, the big, wild sheep recently re-introduced into these mountains from Corsica. At this time of year, Amelia told me, they most often move in groups of three; the mother with the one lamb from last year and the one from this year. The fathers, apparently, were away on the very high tops, surplus to requirements and sulking. At last, the threesome settled for the night in a copse of alder, a signal to us all that the day was done.

The sleeping arrangements were simple; Jean-Marie, Amelia and Grandma would sleep in one chalet, the girls in another and the boys in a third. Apparently, I was one of the boys. We would sleep on the floor, but that was no great hardship; the youngsters treated me as their guest of honour and presented me with two mattresses, the only pillow and the prime location beside the window.

Chapter Two

Cheese-Tasting for England

The night passed without disturbance in a loft dormitory with six teenage boys. They had made not the slightest sound, either going to bed or at any time during the night. I only hoped they could say the same about me.

I was faced with the prospect of a hungry morning. I had eaten all my bread and cheese the night before and had nothing left for breakfast. Jean-Marie came up trumps yet again. With the flourish of a magician, he produced a solitary teabag. Not just an ordinary teabag, but a special green tea, grapefruit-flavoured teabag. I do not drink tea; nothing would induce me to drink it at home, regardless of its greenness or its grapefruitiness. But, early in the morning on a high mountainside, hot grapefruit-flavoured green tea is delicious – even if a little lacking in bulk!

Jean-Marie would take nothing for providing me with a bed, nor for the excellent wine, not even for the sachet of green tea. I am an old-fashioned Englishman, by George, so I was embarrassed by this situation and really wanted to pay my way. Something in his eyes told me that he would be offended if I pressed him further, so I swallowed my pride and accepted his generosity; the age-old, genuine hospitality of hill-folk to travellers. How quickly even an old Englishman can adapt.

The whole extended family, Grandma and all, turned out to form an honour-guard and cheer me on my way. With their *bonne routes* ringing in my ears I could not have imagined a better start, or a better day. The sky was clear and a deep blue from one horizon to the other. Here, well above the timber line, the slanting sunlight picked out and sharpened every shape and undulation of the rocks. I turned for my last wave to the wonderful happy family in the middle distance and for a last look at a sombre Lake Geneva still brooding moodily on the far horizon. I had a short, sharp climb up to the ridge and then a long, gentle climb down the other side to arrive at the Refuge de Bise.

I kicked the goats off the chairs and sat down to a splendid *al fresco* breakfast. I may have been in the middle of nowhere, but I luxuriated with a highly-civilised, true French *petit dejeuner*: a steaming bowl of coffee, chunks of fairly fresh bread, big dollops of butter and a variety of home-made jams. It was a breakfast with a view. The west was still dominated by the spectacular outline of the Dent d'Oche; by now, I had almost walked right round it. To the east, the craggy ridge of Les Cornettes de Bise rose like the skeletal hand of a corpse clawing itself up from the grave. The two rock outcrops appeared like a giant portico through which puny, ant-sized figures of walkers enter to begin their long GR5 walk south.

Licking my lips of the last vestiges of jam, I left the Refuge and followed the path up a rocky outcrop. A small colony of marmots were playing in the rocks and on the scree below. Marmots are daft, comical creatures, well worth watching. This group reminded me of playtime at primary school; a great deal of energy expended to no great effect. Absorbed by their own games of tag they ignored me as I plodded past with a chuckle.

Reaching the top of a ridge in the Alps is like watching a scene-change in the theatre. The foreground safety-curtain slowly rises to reveal the magnificence of the new backdrop. Like a child at a pantomime, I find myself holding my breath in sheer wonderment at the change as the whole panoramic view becomes visible. So it was on the col at Pas de la Bosse. The backcloth was that massive wall of Swiss mountains, the Dents du Midi, which form a high cliff topped with a series of conical peaks of roughly equal height. From this distance it looked like a giant's castle and it was a scene that made my heart thump with sheer joy. The full splendour and scale of those cliffs and towers would become more apparent as I get closer. I could expect some very fine walking in the next day or two with that scenery urging me onwards.

The col was a suitable spot to test out my sat-nav equipment. I prefer to call it my Cosmic Friend. How on earth has mankind reached the point where we can develop an advanced, sophisticated technology such as the Global Positioning System and yet can only describe it in such inadequate language as 'sat-nav'? If there is an uglier word in the English language, I have yet to meet it. The word has all the glamour of a lavatory cleaner.

In the UK, my pocket Cosmic Friend gives my precise location by Ordnance Survey map reference. It can be a life-saver when lost in the Lake District or in a snowstorm in the Cairngorms. Alas, it is next to useless in France. The latest French IGN Walkers' Maps are splendid in every respect, except that, although they claim to be GPS-compatible, they are far from GPS-friendly. The GPS instrument-reading received in France relates not to the grid-lines boldly printed over the map, but to a second grid which has no printed grid-lines and is only referenced by a few, small numbers on the sides of the map. This is a problem. If I lay the map out flat on the dining room table and use two T-squares I can transfer the instrument reading from the numbers on the edge to a location on the map in a twinkling. Sitting on that col, I just could not keep the map flat or still for long enough to project two lines from the edges to intersect at a position somewhere near the centre. The weather was fine, the sun shining and only a light breeze blowing. I seldom get lost in my dining room, or when the sun is shining.

I get lost in atrocious weather, with the snow threatening to bury me just before the wind blows me over a cliff. Any map that I remove from its waterproof case in those conditions is going to be a sodden pulp in seconds; its tattered remnants blowing away before there is the slightest chance of working out precisely where I am. Reluctantly, I packed away my Cosmic Friend and mentally pensioned him off. In France in mid-summer I am likely to be safe enough with a map folded in its case and my trusty compass in my hand.

Beyond the col, the route disappeared into a quagmire of mud. There had been torrential rains two days before. 'Very unnormal rains!' local walkers twice assured me. There were large landslides and soggy mud slips crossing the route at all angles. I made a muddy and slippery descent. In a crisis, the trivial seems to oust the serious from my mind. I was determined not to fall; I concentrated all of my efforts on precisely where I placed my feet and I transferred my weight with the utmost caution. I should have been exercising all this care to avoid the high probability of twisting an ankle because that would have been the end of my whole expedition. But I was not; my mind was working on an entirely different plane, on something that seemed far more important to me at the time. I only had one pair of shorts and I did not want to walk for the next two weeks with a dirty backside. In the event, my entirely illogical thinking caused no upset and I walked on with sound ankles and clean shorts.

The village of La Chapelle d'Abondance is worth the effort required to reach it. It is so perfect, so obviously in accord with one's ideal of an alpine village. Impressive chalets line both sides of the spacious main street. The chalets are capped by overhanging, low-pitched roofs. Balconies and verandas jut out at every conceivable opportunity and at every angle. Hanging baskets and window boxes dripping with flowers of every colour smother whole elevations. I sat down for a beer, closed my eyes and waited for the sound of music.

The Abondance Valley is a popular ski resort in the winter, and if I had my way I would shower its Mayors and Town Planners with garlands and gold medals. Most ski resorts are dreadful places to pass through in summer; ugly scabs on the landscape. Those responsible for the numerous resorts that disfigure the landscape across the Pyrenees and the Alps should visit the Abondance Valley. No concrete apartment blocks brutalise the skyline here. No modern buildings overwhelm the small houses of the original village. In this valley, no piles of rusting iron scrap, of old pylons or of crashed cable cars litter approaches to villages that were beautiful before the invasion of the neon glitz of the ubiquitous pizza bars and coffee shops. This valley wants the economic benefits of the ski-ing industry, but, at the same time, insist that any development is built in harmony with the traditional local architecture. If only others would follow their example.

Strolling through the holiday throng in the main street, I could tell from a hundred yards off that the two back-packers coming towards me were British. I had read the subtle signs right, and soon I was shaking hands with two Scotsmen who introduced themselves, with no irony, as the Scottish Saints. Luke was a giant hewn from his native Aberdeen stone. It is difficult for granite blocks to smile and he managed to speak without moving his head or permitting either his eyes or his lips to show the slightest quiver of emotion. Yet I warmed to him instantly because he somehow gave off likeable vibes. In contrast, Andrew was standard-sized with a shock of curly black hair and a grin. What a grin! He broke into the warmest, broadest smile at the least opportunity and when Andrew smiled birds sang, church-bells rang and the sun shone. With the right manager, that smile would have been worth a fortune. If they had not claimed to be the Scottish Saints, I would have nicknamed them David and Goliath, so marked was the contrast between them. They had chosen to carry camping equipment and were lugging backpacks weighing well over 70 lbs. With their backs bowed under the load, they looked like snails in a funeral procession. It had taken them three days to get here from St Gingolph because of that weight and because they been caught in those 'very unnormal' rains. To my certain knowledge, they humped those enormous weights from St Gingolph to Chamonix for eight days – and they did not camp once! If you want to enjoy the mountains, my advice is to carry less than 20 lbs on your back.

The easy-going half of me wanted to loiter and savour the pleasures of La Chapelle all the afternoon. The conscientious half considered that it was too early in the trip to take an afternoon off; after all, I had only been walking for two half-days. Perhaps some Calvinistic draft was blowing from Switzerland in the mountain air because, totally out of character, the conscientious half prevailed and I decided to walk on. Not before I had enjoyed my lunch. Salad Niçoise is delicious almost anywhere in France; washed down with a glass of the local Chardonnay X Jacqueline and finished with a plate of Abondance cheese, it is a gourmet's delight in the Haute Savoie. The Abondance cheese is a soft, creamy, pale yellow concoction developed by the monks of the local Abbey some seven hundred years ago. These monks were fundamentalists. They started from first principles by developing their own breed of cow, the Abondance, then, a century or two later, they moved on to perfect their cheese. I walked on in monkish meditation, on the look out for that ancient breed of cow.

Grand Randonée footpath routes throughout France are signposted by a small rectangular emblem of horizontal stripes, white over red, similar to the flag of Poland. Unusually, the flags directed me along a well-trafficked road for a couple of miles before they took pity on me and directed me to turn off on to footpaths leading south, across the Abondance River and up onto the wooded flanks of the magnificent Mont de Grange; the next serious mountain on the route.

It was early afternoon and bright, and yet in a clearing in the heavy woodland, there was a bat busily flitting from point to point. Did this nocturnal creature realise that it was cavorting in daylight and presenting an obvious target to its enemies? Which made me wonder; if a bat navigates by radar and cannot see, then how on earth does it know whether it is night or day?

The mudslides and footpaths were just as bad on this side of the valley. Relying confidently on the efficacy of my waterproof socks, I plodded flat-footed up the middle of the path, regardless of the depth of the mud, soon looking like a mud-wrestler from the knees down. I did not care; my feet were dry and my backside was, as far as I could tell, more or less unblemished. Once I had reached the tree line, I was stunned by the panorama of the Mont de Grange which opened up before me. On this, its north side, the flank of the mountain forms a gigantic arena, the Cirque de Mattes; an impressive curved bowl of an escarpment some three thousand feet high and about half a mile in diameter. Here, on the edge of the bowl, I could now see my night's lodging-place. The few huts of Refuge Trebentaz, on the other side of the bowl and about half way up towards its rim, looked small and remote but they had the allure and mystique of a Tibetan monastery perched on a cliff-face. Shangri-La was in sight and I wanted to be there. The final zigzag climb round and up the curve of the bowl along treacherous, muddy paths on tired legs was gruelling. I gave up any attempt to keep my clothes clean and just trudged with my head down. To keep my mind occupied, I cursed in as many languages as I could. After what seemed an age, I arrived at the Refuge and placed myself at the mercy of Madame. So serene was she in the midst of a mayhem of scrumming walkers that I called her Madame la Reine. She seemed pleased enough at the promotion and gave me a cold beer. I washed that day's clothes and took a cold shower (noticeably colder than the beer). Refreshed, I felt on top of the world – which I nearly was. Well, not quite; but at five thousand feet I was higher than anywhere or anyone in Britain.

I like eating in Refuges. Madame la Reine cheerfully brought enough food to provision an army. She brought it in huge bowls which she placed in the middle of the tables so that we could serve ourselves. This sharing of pie and swapping dishes of vegetables immediately got strangers talking. Nobody eats alone in a Refuge, everyone has somebody to talk to. This evening I was Mother, and ladled out bowlfuls of soup from giant tureens for a family of four. The family in question was the memorable Famille Martinet from Alsace; father Bernard, mother Cecilia and daughters Colette and Christelle. With such beautiful names I was not sure whether I was meeting a family or the cast of an opera.

The girls were young to be climbing in the mountains and I was reminded of my seven-year-old grand-daughter who wanted to climb a mountain in Scotland with Grandpa. Concerned about the stamina of one so young, I thought it best to start with something gentle and chose Catbells in the Lake District for her initiation. At the bottom of the mountain I gave Eva the benefit of my accumulated wisdom.

'Start slowly, sweetheart. Stop as often as you like.'

So she started slowly and stopped every few minutes. Very soon, she lost patience with that idea and ran all the way up the mountain, leaving me plodding up behind. Crueller members of my family now refer to Catbells as 'Come on Grandpa Mountain'.

All four Martinets were eager to improve their English but their natural good manners restrained them from bombarding me with too many questions at once. The youngest had the least inhibition and, looking me in the eye, she asked, to the slight discomfort of her parents,

'What is the name of your wife?'

'Jo,' I replied.

'Where is she?'

The parents were distinctly embarrassed and fluttered with quiet admonitions. Still, it was a fair question and I replied,

'She is at our home in England. She prefers to enjoy our garden in the summer rather than carry weights up mountains.'

The parents quickly directed the conversation to their house in Alsace. They were school teachers and the children appeared to enjoy every subject in school (surely my poor French had failed me). They were a friendly family and excellent dinner companions. Until, that is, I discovered their fanaticism for cheese.

Walking alone has its pros and cons. The main disadvantage is having nobody else to blame when things go wrong. The advantages stem from pleasing yourself and meeting strangers. I have walked the French mountains singly and in parties of two and three. The other walkers in a Refuge or a gîte generally welcome one walker, particularly an old fogey with grey hair and stuttering French. Two walkers they regard as a self-contained unit and treat them politely enough, but leave them to themselves. A party of three walkers is an entirely different matter. You can sense the French thinking, 'There are too many Englishmen here'.

The paradox of walking alone is that it is the easiest way of getting to know people. Way up in the rarefied air of a remote Refuge, strangers are often happy to tell me their life history. I do not know why it is, but they open up as if they are in the confessional. Perhaps a greybeard, mumbling incoherently and sipping alcohol, stirs some old memory of the priest in them. More likely, they are teasing me with porkies.

As the Martinets chattered on, the sun gave us our own *son et lumière* display, starkly highlighting the ridge against the evening sky as it set behind the great mass of Mount Grange. By the soup course, there, in stark silhouette, was a stag chamois daintily picking his way up the ridge followed by his harem of does and that year's herd of youngsters. Poised, elegant and delicate they looked so beautiful in relief – which was more than could be said for the cause of this cavalcade. By the meat course, two climbers had appeared, clambering up the same ridge and unwittingly driving the chamois before them. Also in silhouette, hunched backs exaggerated by rucksacks, legs and walking-poles jutting at all angles, the climbers ponderously made for the peak and the considerable prize of its wide-angle views in the sunset. Poised and elegant they were not. Another zillion years of evolution and perhaps *Homo sapiens* will look as natural on the mountain tops as the chamois do today. Or perhaps not.

Meanwhile, back at the dinner table, the Martinets talked cheese. From father to nine-year old Christelle they were happiest discussing cheese, and young Colette even took notes. I have a limited vocabulary when it comes to discussing cheese in English; I am practically mute on the subject in French. Regardless of the language difficulties, they were eager to know my opinion of the cheeses being served. Napoleon must have decreed the cheese course – it is surely embedded somewhere in the French constitution. It does not matter where you are in France or how few stars your hotel has, there will be a cheese selection served between the meat course and the pudding. We were in a Refuge so inaccessible that Madame la Reine winched up supplies by cable from the valley below, and yet still she served a generous cheese course. My cheese-mad friends really wanted my detailed opinion of each of the six cheeses on the plate, but since, to them, I was inarticulate they accepted, after due negotiation, that I should simply rank the cheeses in order of preference. The chatter of the girls and the passing of the cheeses had attracted the attention of the entire dining room. An audience stood intently behind me. This had become a serious matter. I felt I was cheese-tasting for England. Assuming an air of seriousness and concentration, I nibbled each cheese in turn. Unfamiliar with the etiquette, I was not sure if I should spit out each mouthful after sampling, like whisky. I have never in my life spat out good whisky and, seeing no suitable receptacle in sight, I swallowed my cheese, hoping I was not thereby disgracing myself or my country. Most of the six cheeses were bland goat and sheep cheeses so, being a man who prefers the strong, smelly blues of Gorgonzola and Stilton, I knew I would have to bluff.

The regional cheese, the Abondance, I had already savoured over lunch. Madame had made one of the goat cheeses (presumably, in her spare time when she was not busy hauling

21

provisions up by cable). There was one wrapped and labelled *fromage de chèvre*; a pinkish-white Chevrotin. My taste buds have been brutalised by a lifetime's fondness for hot curry and even hotter lime pickle so I have long lost the subtle, gustatory skills needed to distinguish between goat and sheep cheese. I had no chance of picking out Madame's cheese. Perhaps this was a case where diplomacy and discretion were more important than the truth. With no regard to flavour or preference, I placed the Abondance first, then the Chevrotin, indicating that the remaining cheeses were in equal third place. With a sigh of relief I realised that this was a judgement of Solomon which met with the tacit, if not ecstatic, approval of all.

Cheese-tasting apart, the first full day had not been too testing, but I still harboured one nail-biting fear of this walk. It was not so much whether I could carry my pack, nor whether I could make the climbs, nor even whether I could cover the distances required. A far bigger fear overshadowed all of these – would I snore in the dormitory?

Once in the mind, a fear wiggles and worms around and cannot easily be dispelled. What if I snore and nobody tells me? So, on that first night in a crowded, mixed-sex dormitory I buried myself in my sleeping bag determined not to snore. I was so determined, so concentrated on the task in hand that I worried myself into a state of full consciousness. I lay there, restless and turning, the hours slowly ticking by. I then began to worry how I could climb mountains in the morning if I did not get some sleep tonight. Then I remembered I had some herbal sleeping pills in my pack which would surely do the trick. But it is not done to put the light on in the middle of the night in a mixed-sex dormitory! I would have to find the tablets in the dark.

So I lay there and wrestled with the next problem. I knew the whereabouts of the sleeping-tablets in my pack; they were in a zipped pocket of my toilet bag. Everything in its place and a place for everything. But all the pills were in the same place; pills for

22

sore throats, as well as those for diarrhoea and constipation – all similarly pressure-wrapped in small foil sheets. How could I locate the right tablets in the dark when I could not remember which pill was which shape? What if I took the wrong ones? How long would the laxative take to wreak havoc?

Small worries balloon into insurmountable problems in the middle of the night and I lay there tormented by these issues. Finally, in the dark, I made my move. I felt for my rucksack, unzipped the right-hand side-pocket, took out my toilet-bag, unzipped the pill compartment, and picked out two round ones! I swallowed them and fell back utterly exhausted by the mental strain. I had picked the right pills, and slept the sleep of the innocent for several hours. At breakfast I could detect no barely-concealed sniggers from the Martinets and so I presumed that I had not snored.

Chapter Three

Onion Soup without the Onion

Graham has a quite-spoken manner, a diffident charm and a neatly manicured beard. I knew immediately that he was a Professor, although his wife Alice had to fill me in on the details. He is a Professor in the Mechanical Engineering Faculty at Reading University and he specialises in combustion, which was about the only burning issue that we did not get round to discussing. Alice was a walking computer. Before she had left England she had absorbed every known fact about the GR5 between Lake Geneva and Chamonix. Hills, heights, distances, Refuges, gîtes, hotels – all details were filed neatly in Alice's brain and a key word unleashed a torrent of information; sorted, accurate, pertinent and precise. It is not surprising that Graham just walked and talked, leaving the thinking and organising to Alice, his walking Google. We had met the previous evening at Refuge Trebentaz when I had opened my map and guidebook to examine the possibilities for the morrow. I should have saved my energy. Alice told me all I wanted to know, and slightly more.

The three of us set off together. We made an easy climb around the inside of the bowl of the Cirque de Mattes and mounted a small, zigzag staircase of rocks to gain the rim. As we reached the very high grassland I was surprised to see small, scattered herds of cattle still using these remote pastures for summer grazing. Occasionally, herds passed us, on their way to pastures new. Practically every cow had a bell round its neck, each a slightly different note. Like wind-chime music, there is neither rhythm nor reason to the sound of a moving herd of cows, but it is a delight to the ear all the same.

The Dents du Midi were closer now and to their south were the first views of the Dents Blanches, the aptly named mountains of gargantuan, white fangs separated by massive glaciers. These were not the pristine, sparkling white, glaciers of a winter's day as seen in the ski-ing adverts; these were the dour, menacing ice-flows in their dirty-grey, late-summer clothes. The mountains themselves soar above the glaciers in disdainful superiority; mile upon mile of rocky crags, sheer rock faces and high screes which set my nerves tingling, so awe-inspiring was the sight.

It must have been the dour, unfriendly surroundings that put us in the frame of mind to talk politics. Perhaps we should instead have responded to the soul-stimulating aspects and discussed something more uplifting. In any case, I did not find it easy holding up my end of a serious conversation with an erudite professor while panting uphill or slipping and sliding downwards.

He opened the debate with a controversial challenge.

'The political parties have stolen our democracy, making us politically impotent.'

'How so?' I asked, slipping on a cowpat two yards behind. Well into his stride, verbally and physically, he continued to explain that one little cross in a box every four or five years was not meaningful power since it gave no significant voice on anything. Not when that single cross had to express his views on war or peace, education, health, taxation, police, Europe, etc. Not when that

25

one cross, in reality, confined him to choosing between one party leader and another. Not when those leaders ignored the fundamental issues. I drew enough breath to suggest that it was even worse, because the political parties, once elected, failed to deliver what they had promised, but instead concentrated on measures previously they had been careful not to mention.

'They didn't tell me they were going to tax my pension fund,' I chipped in cheerfully. We marched shoulder to shoulder in walkers' solidarity; entirely in step and egging each other on with revolutionary fervour. If Lech Walesa had beckoned, we would have followed.

We continued debating with great fervour, ready at any moment to mount the barricades. Graham was in favour of the Swiss model where the politicians are unashamedly professional careerists. The difference between the Swiss model and ours lies in the way the politicians approach the electorate. In Switzerland, he said, politicians do not claim to be super-managers but they do explain the various aspects of a wide range of issues to an electorate which then considers and votes on each one. During the five years between our ineffectual little crosses, the Swiss voter expresses his opinions with votes on thirty different issues. Not only is Switzerland a functioning democracy it is also a peace-loving neutral state. In accord, Graham and I recognised that there was a strong connection between the two. After all, Switzerland was not fighting in Iraq. The motion was that 'Political Parties are the Pits'. In the first debate of the Trebentaz Debating Society the motion was carried unanimously

I looked again to the Dents du Midi across the valley in Switzerland and thought that perhaps the glaciers on that side were purer and brighter than I had first appreciated.

Today's walk looked extremely arduous on those graphs of altitude and distance so popular with mountain guidebook editors. Today's graph showed a path that climbed a series of ridges and each looked to have a gradient so steep as to require Sherpas and ropes. But the graph exaggerates, it squashes the horizontal scale yet stretches the vertical. Nor did it take into account the design of the path and, as I found on the first day, the careful gradations of the zig-zags can make climbing even a steep mountain a relatively easy stroll. Today, in spite of those wicked-looking graphs the walking was easy. True enough, the route crossed four ridges but the paths between them were gentle and I could manage them without stops for breathers – more than can be said for the previous two days. Perhaps I was getting fitter, although I could still find use for a Sherpa.

Much of the walk was on the level through woodland with birds of all kind around us. Under the tree canopy, I saw a large black bird fly ahead of me along the track. Walk slowly, tread quietly, watch carefully. Yes! There just ahead, was a large woodpecker doing what woodpeckers do best, showing itself off in profile, walking vertically up a tree and banging its beak on the trunk for the sheer fun of it. As big as a rook and as just as black, but with a signatory crown of crimson, the Black Woodpecker is unmistakeable. It has recently spread west across France although it has yet to be seen in Britain and for me such a clear sighting was a great thrill.

By lunchtime, the three founding members of the Trebentaz Debating Society had reached the Swiss-French border. This time, there were no armed policemen or glowering customs-officers. A chef with a white apron, a cheerful grin and a well-stocked kitchen was in command. If only all border posts could be the same, places of friendly reception rather than of hostile interrogation and refusal. The Professor and his wife were anxious to push on and reach the hotel they had booked in a ski resort slightly off the route and just over the horizon. That forced me to choose between further political debate and a plate of omelette and chips. Five minutes later, I washed the chips down with a glass of ice-cold bottled beer, watching the Professor and his Google toiling up the opposite hillside. Their efforts looked so strenuous that I had another beer. Sufficiently re-fuelled I strode into Switzerland. It was time to consider my accommodation options but I was undecided whether to stay on the Swiss side or pass over the next col back into France. There seemed to be plenty of small Refuges so I decided that I would just walk until evening and make my choice later.

I came upon a couple who had everything. They were wearing or carrying something from every shelf of an up-market outdoor activity shop. Every item of clothing sported a well-known designer-label and was in this year's colours. Those poor snails had such large shells on their backs that they could hardly crawl. Naturally, they were both paid-up members of the drip-feed brigade. Quite why fit and able-bodied people need to walk along continuously suckling a plastic tube connected to a water container in their rucksack is beyond my comprehension. Are they chronically incontinent? Why else do they need to drink water continuously? With my system, or lack of it, the odd sip of water is a treat, a rare event to be celebrated, creating opportunities for self-motivation.

'Get your lazy body beyond that next fir tree on the left and you can have a swig.'

'Keep going for another five minutes and you can have a drink break.'

In this way, I can cheat and cajole myself all the way up a mountain and at the top enjoy a sip of water which then has all the taste and sparkle of a glass of vintage champagne.

Nor can I understand the modern craze for walking poles. They must get in the way half the time, and in the other half – what are they for? When I am walking I like to adjust the length and speed of my pace to the situation, just as a cyclist needs to change gears. Going up a steep hill, I drop into crawl gear and force myself to walk just fast enough not to fall over backwards. When the climb is really steep, I want both hands free to pull on rocks or branches. Once I am on the level, I find it easy enough to click into cruise control and walk at a steady, comfortable stride without any need for a regimental swagger stick. Downhill can be tricky. Sometimes the easiest way down a steep, smooth gradient is to run slowly with knees bent outwards. This is the most inelegant form of locomotion so far devised by the human race, but it is a highly effective way to get down hillsides. I learned it from a porter in Borneo and I call it the Kinabalu trot in his honour. It does have the disadvantage of significantly increasing the internal pressure on the bladder, but since it compensates by getting you to the privacy of the tree line more quickly it is not much of a problem. Sometimes the downhill surface is too slippery or irregular to trot and so I control my speed by walking emphatically flat-footed, as though I was wearing flippers. In this mode I look slightly more elegant – more like an elderly walrus lolloping hopefully after its mate. Finally, there are those situations where the descent is so steep that I need to use both hands to hold on. In most of these conditions two poles would be a nuisance, so I am happy to walk with hands free.

By late afternoon, I realised that I had time to cross back into France but I still had an appetite for all things Swiss. And, as if to order, there at La Pierre was the iconic Swiss chalet, with its balconies and flowers, offering sustenance and rest to passers-by. I wouldn't have been surprised if a cuckoo had popped out of an upstairs window as the hour struck. Inside, I received more hot coffee than I could drink, more cream cake than I could guzzle and more advice than I could absorb. I enquired if there were any Refuges within a couple of hours walk ahead.

'Ah yes,' was the consensus opinion of the waitress, the cook, two shepherds and a big man with a huge, Lord Kitchener moustache.

'Ah yes. There are three Refuges quite close together, just over the border, but the best one is Chalet de Freterolle.'

Grateful for their generous refreshment, knowledgeable advice and friendly good wishes, I walked on towards the Border at the Col de Coux.

The weather had deteriorated by the time I crossed into Switzerland. By late afternoon it was raining and windy, so I took out my waterproof poncho. Why are rain ponchos so popular on the continent and yet seldom seen on our rainy islands? They are cheap and practical. As soon as rain-clouds loom I pull mine out from a convenient outer pocket of my rucksack and I carry it ready in my hand. Once the rain starts I can pull it over both me and my rucksack without stopping. By contrast, the poor anorak-wearer has to stop, take-off his rucksack, put on his anorak, fumble over zips with cold fingers and then put his rucksack back on before he can start walking again. On a showery day, with my poncho I will reach the pub hours before him – and with a dry rucksack. But it does not do to be too smug, especially if there are tears in your poncho. As the wind picked up, I held tight to the poncho flaps. Gusts pulled at the tears and eventually ripped the cape apart at the seams. I was left holding the corners of useless tatters of plastic which streamed in the wind. Exposed to the elements, I swore that in future I would avoid bargain basements.

I was wet to the skin and, with the sharp wind, very cold. There was no point in putting on an extra layer. It would soon be saturated, I would be no warmer and I would have nothing in reserve. I had no option but to walk as fast as I could to keep warm and get to a shelter as quickly as possible. Perhaps I should have brought anti-pneumonia tablets instead of those useless laxatives!

The cols in this immediate vicinity are at the outer limits of Les Dents Blanches, which themselves form the extreme western corner of the Alps. That geography makes them significant staging points on the migratory routes of many species of birds and there is intense study of their movements by both Swiss and French scientists. The Swiss Ornithological Society has its own dedicated research building on the Col de Coux. It was still raining when I got there, so I sheltered for a few moments in the Ornithological Porch to preen my bedraggled self while I made my final plan. The rain must have soaked into my brain, because I decided to ignore the informed opinion of the entire population of La Pierre and go to Refuge Chardonniere. According to the map, it was marginally closer to the route than Chalet de Freterolle. How stupid could I be?

Immediately beyond the col, the path descended steeply and the rain had turned it into a dangerous slide. I slithered down the treacherous track as best I could, falling over more than once. So much for trying to keep a clean backside. Back on the col I had met three mountain bikers. They were friendly enough, but what a mess their bikes had made on a difficult, already slippery, track. There is a move afoot among the committees of various Wilderness and National Parks around the world to ban mountain bikers. Is this really necessary? Do cyclists cause that much more erosion than walkers? I have dispassionately thought through this whole issue at home and come to the conclusion that we should be tolerant and open the wilderness to all who respect and appreciate their surroundings. On the way down that mountainside, wet to the skin, shivering with cold and slip-sliding down a churned-up muddy track, tolerance was in short supply. I swore loudly, cursing equally and emphatically shoddy poncho manufacturers and mountain bikers, however friendly.

I arrived at Refuge Chardonniere with all the sartorial elegance of a drowned marmot and asked for a bed for the night. Madame, warm and dry in her cosy kitchen, faced me, hands on hips, and with no flicker of compassion, told me that the Refuge was '*complet*'. That one word appeared to be the sum total of her vocabulary. In another age she would have been knitting beside a guillotine. Her tone and body language left not the slightest expectation of further dialogue, so I turned away to consult my map and plan my route to somewhere else, anywhere else! A shy Mademoiselle appeared with somewhat more grace and warmth than Madame (an ice-cube has more warmth than Madame).

'But we have a tent,' she said.

I inspected a large, four-person tent with mattresses. Since Mademoiselle assured me that I would have it all to myself, I took it. An all-male hayloft, a mixed dormitory and now a single-occupancy tent; what might tomorrow bring?

As I took an extremely cold shower, I tried to remember what it was like to be just slightly warm. Afterwards, I was able to put on some dry clothes and I draped myself in my sleeping bag to regain some body warmth. The chair is an artefact of civilisation that has yet to reach this remote outpost of the Haute Savoie, so I wrote my daily notes squatting cross-legged in my tent like a genuine bedouin sheikh. When I emerged from my tent at about 7 o'clock, sniffing for a beer, I passed a dozen men wearing crash helmets and carrying heavy coils of rope over their shoulders. They were gone into the gloom of a wet evening before I could find out whether they were moonlight mountaineers or whether we were in a pot-holing area. Their presence, or rather their absence, did perhaps explain how it was that I had my dinner with Madame in an empty dining-room in a Refuge that was 'full'.

Mademoiselle had disappeared so I sat with Madame at a large wooden table designed to seat twenty. She grunted rather than spoke, which made translation simple. She smoked continuously throughout the meal, with considerable dexterity. So interwoven were her operations of eating and smoking that it seemed inevitable that she would confuse the two. Surely at some stage she would chew her cigarette and draw lustily on a forkful of potato. She never did.

The legerdemain of my hostess made some slight compensation for the boredom of the dreadful meal. We started with what she announced in a grunt to be French Onion Soup. Not normally the choice of a man who prefers the strong flavours of mulligatawny or ox-tail, but I thought onion soup might be better on its home ground. Looking at it, a colourless liquid with no redeeming features like cheese or croutons, was bad enough. Tasting it, a colourless liquid without even an onion to redeem it, was even worse. I supped slowly and managed to maintain a weak smile and the occasional grunt of conversation the while. It was enough for her. Continuous assault by hot smoke had totally anaesthetised her taste-buds, but I was old-fashioned enough still to prefer a vestige of flavour with my food.

The main course was potato and andouillette, which is a sausage made exclusively from the unmentionable parts of a pig. By comparison with the rest of the meal, the ordinary mashed potato, bereft of butter as it was, seemed a gourmet's heaven. The andouillette was well-nigh uneatable. Gristle outnumbered meat by a ratio of about ten to one. Uncooked gristle, cuddling up to globs of white stomach-lining, made the rare crumbs of red meat look possibly palatable: a cruel deception. In hunger, I wiped every last molecule of potato from my plate and pushed the pig's unmentionables to one side, mumbling some falsehood about being vegetarian as an excuse for my behaviour.

Moonlighting mountaineering was evidently not the explanation for the empty dining-room. At 8.30 p.m., a cavalcade of about twenty, dripping-wet, horse-trekkers arrived. Male and female were indistinguishable – all wore oversized, long-flared waterproof coats and broad-rimmed felt hats, reminding me of those old films of Australian sheep drovers 'in the wet'. To give them their due, they had taken care of the horses first, tethering them out in the field with a nosebag of oats as some consolation for their discomfort in the rain. When the party took over the Refuge, I retired to what I imagined would be the quiet cocooned seclusion of my tent.

I was much more comfortable than either the trekkers or their horses. My tent was warm and dry and there was far more privacy and peace than in any dormitory. On the other hand, I was in the middle of a field, outside it was raining heavily and there were cows munching all around. Alone in that tent in the dark, reality began to warp again. Outside noises became magnified inside the tent, and as I lay there I realised that cows only have two functions, one at each end, both equally noisy and both almost continuous. The rain became harder, the noises off got louder and closer. I began to wonder whether I would be chewed to death, drowned in floodwater or asphyxiated by something worse. I fell asleep in the middle of my speculations and woke in the morning unscathed.

I breakfasted while the cavalry still slept and made my escape early in the morning. The next time I am passing by that neck of the woods I will follow the advice of the locals and try the Chalet de Freterolle.

Chapter Four

The Good Duke Amadeus

I quickly regained the ridge above Chardonnière and a brisk walk brought me to the Col de la Golese. It was quiet and abandoned at this time of year. In the spring and autumn it bustles with activity, a throbbing international hub, with birds coming in from a wide arc to the south and flying off over an equally wide arc to the north. The cols in the area teem, not only with the thousands of birds passing through, but with large numbers of ornithologists, both professional scientists and amateur tickers and twitchers, trying to record all the comings and goings.

A small bird crossing this enormous mountain range would know that this Col is the lowest crossing point for miles around. It would know instinctively because it is descended from a long line, from hundreds of generations of birds who have been clever, or lucky, enough to find that narrow passage and gain the Promised Land on the other side. Those forebears quickly celebrated their good fortune by breeding enthusiastically and passing on their successful genes. I find it almost impossible to believe, yet by some miraculous process, those genes include a navigation system which will get their descendants to the Col de la Golese from all points of the compass from Leningrad to Lithuania, from Egypt to Espagne. Those small birds have evolved their own GPS that totally outclasses my own Cosmic Friend, for all its high-tech sophistication and billion-dollar satellite back-up.

Each year scientists net, ring and record over a thousand birds on this remote col. Over the past twenty-five years, they have ringed almost one hundred and twenty thousand birds, although only about three thousand have been recovered subsequently. Their work, even with this seemingly low rate of return, has given the ornithologists some fascinating information. For example, hordes of blue tits pass through every year and yet, strangely, coal tits only pass through every other year. I spent two hours walking down from the col trying to think of one good reason for that fact. Since coal tits arrive in England every year to breed, I persuaded myself that there must be two distinct populations of coal tits. The first migrate across Col de la Golese and implant their offspring to do the same. The second population migrate across a different route. But wait, that would require the two populations to know that they were different and not to interbreed. If they did interbreed, the navigation systems of their offspring would blow a fuse and they would get lost on migration. I cast around in my mind for a second hypothesis. All I could come up with was the idea that every coal tit must be born with two navigational routes imprinted in its brain, together with a calendar to tell which route applied each year. It seemed too incredible to accept. I was flummoxed. In the end, I conceded defeat and turned my attention back to the route.

Many people dislike walking downhill more than uphill. Not me. If gravity is going to be kind enough to release me from some of the weight of my body and pack then I am going to take advantage and speed downhill just as quickly as my leg joints and the Kinabalu trot will allow. Once my shorts had dried, walking became more comfortable. I flew down that mountainside into the Giffre Valley and began to consider a long day's hike across the river and up the other side. The windswept moorland of the tops gradually became open meadow with stands of fir. There were a number of jays about. At one point, I counted a family of five in a clearing, flitting around, flaunting their white bottoms and shouting to each other with their distinctively raucous calls.

Fir trees do nothing for me, so I pass them without interest. In Britain, that is understandable. In France, it is a mistake. In Britain, large, commercial forests blanket the landscape with a monotony of colour and form; grown simply for profit, the planters show no concern for their ecological impact. I can find little joy in walking along the straight line of a fire-break in a British plantation. Invariably, there is only one species of fir, tightly-packed in rows to the detriment of most other living things (except legions of midges). Here on the tree line, I realised that I should not carry my prejudices across the Channel to France. In the Alps, a variety of coniferous trees are indigenous, they seed themselves where they will, and they prosper where they are content. As a result, they produce natural landscape groupings in harmony and balance with their environment. I wandered off the track and into the woods to see what I could find. The random and low-density groupings of different types of conifers made for an attractive landscape and I promised myself I would learn more about them.

As I descended, the conifers gave way to beech forest and, though still far from civilisation, the track became better defined. At the very first spot where the track could conceivably be called a road was a car park for walkers setting out to conquer the heights of Les Dents Blanches. I was amazed, in this remote spot, to see the driver of a small van from the local Village Commune de Samoens empty the litter bin. He told me he emptied that bin daily, as well as twelve others in locations equally remote. I was impressed with such civic pride and walked on humming '*La Marseillaise*'.

Samoens at mid-morning in mid-summer is one cheerful carnival. Bunting, flags, table sunshades and flowers splashed brilliant and exuberant colour everywhere. Holidaying families were enjoying the sunshine with their young children. After the solitude of the mountains, the vitality of the crowds gave me a buzz. Whatever thoughts I had about walking on, died a painless death the moment I set foot in that town square. I sat under a sunshade with a beer. I was here for the day, the other side of the valley could wait.

After three days in the wilds, the luxury of my own *en suite* room with a real bed was too tempting to resist. I enquired at the most central Logi hotel. Yes, they had a room, but they also had a problem with their kitchen and could not provide an evening meal. Foolishly, I confirmed my booking when it might have been wiser to look for another hotel. I had made two daft decisions in twenty-four hours. Perhaps, in the thin mountain air, I was suffering from the dreaded COD – cerebral oxygen deficiency! Logis are fun and good value for money, but only on *demi-pension* terms. The Logi owner regards the fixed-menu dinner for the demi-pensioner as the measure of his credibility as a restaurateur. He will go to great lengths to demonstrate to you that he has devised a most interesting menu based on his vast culinary expertise, and influenced by local or regional specialities. He will start by describing the prime ingredient of the main course and he will emphasise how well the sauce and the vegetables complement the main item. Unquestionably, he has selected the starter to prepare your palate. He will suggest that you might enjoy a small pitcher of the local wine, which, of course, he has likewise most carefully chosen for its suitability. It goes without saying that his choice of pudding will bring the whole gastronomic experience to a deeply satisfying and triumphant finale. The French Logi owner proves his manhood and establishes his rank among men by the quality and the originality of his *demi-pension* dinner menu.

I would miss out on Monsieur's delights, but, more importantly, I would lose the opportunity to converse with other guests. I choose to walk at my own pace and make my own plans during the day, but I do like to mix with people in the evenings, preferably an oddball selection of ages, nationalities, interests and eccentricities. A pity I would not meet any here tonight, since a Logi dining-room can be good oddball territory. By way of compensation, I luxuriated under a long, hot shower.

The body cleansed, I gathered my dirty clothes and found the local laundromat. The washing machines were mammoth, big enough to take a month's washing for a family of six. The clothes got the full blast of the industrial-size spin-dryer as well, and I left with every item of clothing clean and dry – if, like their owner, a little wrinkled.

Next, I turned my attention to my pack. I worked on the basis that if I had not used an item in the past three days, I was unlikely to use it during the next fortnight and could safely send it home. The useless camera *sans* battery, the next-to-useless Cosmic Friend, the fourth pair of socks, the map of territory already covered, the book I had read on the plane and the insect repellent were all sent home, unused and unloved. I did keep the two lots of pills. They had been unwanted so far but, could become critically important at any moment.

The purchase of a top-quality poncho completed my housekeeping and I was soon back in the square having a beer. The Scottish Saints passed through but were so determined to make steady progress they would not even stop for a drink. I tried to remember how many years it was since I had walked passed a friendly bar on a sunny day without stopping for a beer. I reckoned it was easily fifty. But then I am not a Saint and I was going to relax and enjoy my afternoon exploring and enjoying all things French in Samoens. Or so I thought.

I sat contentedly enjoying the Samoens carnival until a raucous quartet took the adjacent table and began making enough of a racket to ensure that there was no contemplation or peace within a hundred yards. Robert and Charlotte owned a house locally and lived there for twelve weeks of the year; their friends, Gordon and Susan, were visiting. When in France, I like to meet a wide range of French people, but I can be a bit picky when it comes to the English. I do not travel all the way to the French Alps to discuss the price of houses in Essex. Gordon was roughly my age, and I could sense his competitiveness from the start. There is a breed of Englishman that simply cannot rest until they have told you the value of their house. They hover on the edge of a conversation, clumsily trying to steer it towards the subject of property prices so that they can introduce their house value and smugly establish their high social rank. How long will it be before I go to a function where the lapel badge, in addition to (perhaps even instead of) my name, will display in bold type a printed number – the value of my property and hence my social standing.

After about twenty minutes of chatter, like all Englishmen abroad we had got round to the price of beer. Gordon saw his chance. Sticking his chin out, he said,

'Talking of prices, it may surprise you to know that my house is worth nearly half a million.'

Although I was not entirely sure of the link between the price of a pint in Samoens and a house in Dagenham, I let it go.

'Really?' said I. 'Now that is impressive.'

With his financial status established, Gordon relaxed and became almost likeable. He would have been far happier had he known the value of my house, but he took my silence on the matter as an admission of his superiority.

Real estate out of the way, they became friendly and amusing company over lunch although they could not understand that I could possibly want to explore Samoens on my own. Charlotte thought that her three-minute potted history of the town was enough to satisfy the most inquisitive visitor. They were going sightseeing in the local hills and they insisted I accompany them.

Not wishing to rebuff their kindly-meant invitation, I went along.

Charlotte wanted to show her friends the local beauty spot at the Waterfall de Roguet. It was a twenty minute drive along the Giffre Valley through the strangely-named village of Sixt-fer-Cheval and up into the hills. While we were admiring the cascades, I noticed on a post the small red and white flag of a Randonée. My GR5 passed this spot. Without intending to, I had carried out a motorised recce of my walk tomorrow. I would have to walk very hard to get here in two hours in the morning and now that I knew there was such an easy road route, the devil set to work in my head.

'Go on,' he said, 'hitch-hike! You know it makes sense!'

In the end, I managed to get some time to myself to explore Samoens. The name is a corruption of the old French for Seven Mountains. In the town's founding charter of 1437, Duke Amadeus VII, Duke of Savoie, granted the local people seven alpine pastures in the surrounding hills. Legend has it that he planted a tree to mark the event. Certainly the most magnificent lime tree, Le Gros Tillent, dominates the town square with its girth of something like thirty-two feet. At that size it must be very ancient, so why not believe it is more than five-hundred years old and that a bizarrely-named Duke, bedecked in feathers and furs, planted it with a silver-spade?

Mention of the Duke of Savoie reminded me that, although I was walking through modern France, my walk would take me through three historic and independent regions, two of which were not part of France until recent times.

The northern part of the walk was through the lands historically ruled by the Counts and Dukes of Savoie. Ruling what are now the modern Departments of Haute Savoie and Savoie, they were thorns in the side of the French for nigh on a thousand years. During that period, the Dukes increased their power by astute diplomacy and strategic marriages. They eventually plotted and bedded themselves down with crowned heads, first of Sicily and then of a united Italy in 1860. Then, in an act of diplomacy that blended generosity with realism, they ceded the Savoies to France in appreciation of the French help in chasing the Austrian Hapsburgs out of Italy.

After the Savoies, I would cross lands known from early times as the Dauphine, reaching up the Isère Valley from Grenoble. Finally, in the South of France I would walk through Provence, once the fiefdom of the Counts of Nice. They, when it suited them, bowed their heads to the King of France or perhaps the King of Sardinia, but mostly were a law unto themselves. The Counts Grimaldi gave up hanging peasants and burning churches some time ago and now live in Monaco as celebrities.

The GR5 would take me through ancient lands which have seen more than their fair share of fighting and squabbling for at least two thousand years and where the present border dates only from 1948. The ruins of military fortifications will litter my route; from first century Roman forts to twentieth century machine-gun emplacements.

Samoens was even more festive in the early evening. A group was singing folk songs in the open-sided market hall, supported by an enthusiastic crowd who joined in the choruses in many tongues. It was the Music Hall of Babel. Many French towns, even quite small ones, have a programme of evening entertainment throughout the summer – another example of French *joie de vivre* and here it was being appreciated by people of all ages and all nationalities. I found an *al fresco* restaurant near enough to hear the music, yet far enough away not to be too disturbed by the choruses. I chose a tasty *tartiflette*, another Savoyard speciality which – what a surprise – is made mostly of cheese. The base is made of potato and the tangy flavour comes from smoked bacon, strong onion and a touch of nutmeg.

I was delighted to be greeted by the other diners as they entered or left the restaurant. The English have a reputation for politeness on the continent (some English, that is, in some parts of Europe). An Italian journalist once famously told his readers that the purchase of

42

a ticket from a conductor on a London bus involved fifteen 'thank yous'. Yet greeting strangers in restaurants is not part of our social repertoire. In France, it is standard practise, whether it is just a nod of the head or the full-blown '*Bon soir, Mesdames-seurs*'.

Chapter Five

The Cheshire Chavs

Early in the morning, the boulangeries and fruiteries of Samoens overflowed with the most tantalising and tempting food. There was bread and cake in every form man could invent, and fruit in every shape and colour that God could devise. With all that temptation, I was peeved that weight considerations limited me to one loaf of bread, a tin of sardines and a chunk of cheese.

With the 'let's hitch-hike' devil cast firmly behind me, I walked out of Samoens. The route follows a disused railway embankment running alongside the river Giffre. The water was that pale, electric blue that tells you it was solid ice a few hours ago and made me shiver just to look at. Ahead, I could just glimpse through the trees Le Point de Sales, a high, rocky pinnacle that stands guard over the Giffre Valley, seeming to protect Sixt and Samoens. The early morning sun reflected off it, flashing as the angle changed, almost as if it were sending me signals, a beacon luring me to the mountains ahead. There were clumps of willows and alders beside the river with flocks of tits flitting from tree to tree ahead of me. Some had the blue-grey tones of blue and great tits but mostly they showed the browner tones of coal, marsh and willow tits. The last two species always confuse me. I cannot tell the difference, even with the aid of binoculars, between those tits with glossy black heads (marsh) and those with dull black heads (willow).

Although a keen bird-watcher, I do not carry binoculars on my walks. In the price range of ordinary mortals, those that are light enough to carry are not strong enough to identify small birds, and those that are good enough are too heavy to carry. But then I never was a ticker. I was quite happy just to have seen a mixed flock of tits; my enjoyment would not have increased had I known precisely how many were of a particular species.

Suddenly a stroll became an adventure. The footpath wound its way through the Gorges les Tines; a sheer-sided canyon about sixty feet deep and seldom more than a few feet wide. Everything was damp and, judging by the amount of exotic ferns and hanging lichens, the place was probably dripping wet for most of the year. It reminded me of the stunningly beautiful Milford Trail on South Island. Even in the early morning, the Gorge was warm, steamy and slightly mysterious. I half expected an aggressive Kea parrot to attack me as I rounded the next bend. There is a series of steel ladders and handrails set out along the route to make progress easier. For a moment I thought I had trespassed into a disused assault course. The steel, rusted and corroded, had surely seen better days, and I tested every rung and rail before entrusting it with something as valuable as my body. Against all reasonable expectation, the metalwork held me for an exhilarating, sometimes hair-raising climb to a perilous ledge with views down into Sixt-fer-Cheval and to the ridges beyond. After that, the route can only go downhill. Normally, nothing irritates me more than having to descend steeply knowing that shortly I will have to work hard to re-gain the height lost. Here, the extra effort was well rewarded by the thrill of the Gorges and the views from the top.

The Waterfall de Roguet somehow looked more interesting this morning when I had taken a couple of hours to reach than it did yesterday when the Dagenham Four had driven me there in a matter of minutes. The waterfalls were higher, the spray caught more light and the rocks were more, well, more rocky. Possibly the physical effort of getting there had heightened my senses; more probably my brain was telling my body, 'You have paid a high price to get here so you had better enjoy it!'

This was Day 5, and in theory I should have been getting fitter, but I found the walk up through the forest hard. I thought I saw yet another jay flit through the trees ahead. The call was not the double screech of the jay but a single, less harsh cry, and alerted by that unusual sound, I looked more carefully and caught another glimpse of the bird in profile. With a thick beak and a dark-coloured body it looked nothing like a jay. Could it be a nutcracker? This is another member of the crow family, about the same size as a jay. A sighting would be an exciting first for me. Nutcrackers are central European birds and I was on the western extremity of its habitat, so I had not expected to see one. I carefully and quietly tiptoe-ed forward in my best impression of the last Mohican. I wanted to be certain and I searched for a second sighting. Jays and nutcrackers both have white rumps which they flaunt conspicuously in flight. There the similarity ends. The jay is dressed for a party in a riot of flamboyant colours from pinks to almost fluorescent blue, whereas the nutcracker is dressed for bed in drab pyjamas of dark brown with white spots. I am fairly certain that my bird was more drab than flamboyant but I never got that second sighting and will never know if I had seen a nutcracker. No, I am *not* a twitcher, but I did make a resolution on the spot: next time I will carry a decent pair of binoculars.

Annoyed by my lack of even elementary knowledge of the trees I saw yesterday, I had bought in Samoens a small French guide to the trees of the Alps which I had struggled late into the night to translate. At least I now knew that two particular coniferous trees dominate in the French Alps; the spruce and the fir. As a general rule, in these mountains, if a tree stands in graceful elegance with its boughs curving gently downwards from its red-tinged trunk then it is a spruce. If it stands stolidly with its branches sticking out akimbo, more or less at right angles to the grey trunk then it is a fir. On this hillside there was a number of very attractive spruce. This is a tree originally from the lowlands of Scandinavia, but after the retreat of the last Ice Age it has crept southwards and established for itself a niche as a mountain-dweller in France. As I had seen, it grows happily right up to the tree line at 6,000 feet.

There were also plenty of stunted firs to set off the delicacy of the spruce. This particular fir has white resin bands on the underside of its needles, which explains why we call it the Silver Fir, although the French prefer to call it the Comb Fir from the arrangement of the needles on its stem. They also call it the Spaniel's Tail for reasons I know not.

Panting a little and dragging heavy legs, I reached the tree line. I was by now on the shoulder of the Point de Sales, that impressive rock which had lured me on earlier that morning. As I rounded the corner it became apparent that the Point de Sales is the northern end of a massive rock wall, the Rochers de Fiz. The rock formation reminded me of the famous Crusader fortress, the Krak de Chevalier. It sits atop a fantastic sweep of scree in Syria, its high defensive wall guarded by stout, circular towers at each end. The Rochers de Fiz must have given the Crusaders the idea in the first place. It has a gigantic rampart of vertical rock some three miles long and about one thousand feet high sitting on rock scree of a further thousand feet in height. Guarding this rampart at either end, the pinnacles of the Point de Sales and the Point d'Anterne add strength and definition to what appeared to me the Fortress of the Gods. When I was in the Syria I found it scarcely believable, although I know it to be true, that Saladin ever conquered the Krak de Chevalier. Here in France, I was sure the Rochers de Fiz would defy even him.

47

Wrenching my gaze southwards, I saw that the Mont Blanc massif was visible for the first time since Lake Geneva. With every step I was getting closer, and now the elusive temptress of the mountains reminded me of her presence by showing that pinkish, bare shoulder, this time behind the curtains of the craggy Massif des Aiguilles Rouges. Lured by that glimpse, I hurried on.

The commonest creatures in the upland pastures of the Alps must be grasshoppers. They are all over the place. As they scattered at my feet it struck me that their evolution is both a triumph and a disaster. The grasshopper has evolved the finest vertical take-off system in the whole of the animal kingdom, leaving the kangaroo trailing when it comes to distance-to-weight ratios. Strong thigh muscles catapult it to a height and distance many times its own body length. Then it all goes haywire; having launched itself so high in the air, evolution lets it down with a thump. For a start, there is no direction control mechanism. Like a bad pilot, it launches itself without bothering to file a flight plan. As often as not the daft thing will jump towards you – not an effective escape mechanism. That is not the end of it. There is no effective landing gear either. I thought of the highly sophisticated technique of a swallow alighting on a telegraph wire, or of a blue tit stalling its flight to land without any forward momentum on the peanut bag. Then I considered the grasshopper; it collapses on its side, or on its back, only occasionally, as if accidentally, on its legs. Its first landing is almost invariably followed by a mad scramble and a second jump in the forlorn hope of landing feet first next time. They must get together now and again for the odd social engagement, there are so many of the wretched things, but how they do it beats me.

As I approached the Refuge d'Anterne I came upon other walkers. The Scottish Saints, those sleep-walking snails with their huge packs and their slow steady plod, told me that they had walked from Sixt this morning. And there, walking the GR5 path, and by this time hours away from any road or suggestion of civilisation, were the two I came to remember affectionately as the Cheshire Chavs. Here we were in the alpine wilderness, and they were dressed for a Caribbean beach party. They could not possibly be walkers; this was not a couple you would expect to meet straying from the path of a city park, let alone off the beaten track and in the high mountains. I was dying for some explanation of their bizarre presence here.

She had a cleavage – not the accidental revelation of a popped-button but a well-displayed, and no doubt expensively acquired cleavage. She was further distinguished by smartly-coiffured hair dyed a startling shade of red. Her unmissable charms were further emphasised by festoons of jewellery. There was bling draped round her neck, coiled round her wrists and dripping from her ears. She spoke in torrents and 'dahlinged' me every second breath she took.

He sported a goatee beard, tattoos, a gold earring and a red tee-shirt over a small but promising beer-belly. I was amazed to learn that they were walking the GR5 from St Gingolph. Earlier on, after I had banished the hitch-hiking devil, it had obviously latched onto them. They had succumbed and taken a taxi from Samoens to Roguet. They turned out to be good walkers and fine company. St Roch should name and shame me for judging them by their appearances.

The Scottish Saints, the Cheshire Chavs and I enjoyed a convivial and first-class lunch at the Refuge d'Anterne. It deserved three-stars by any standards, let alone for a restaurant so remote that it had to be provisioned intermittently by helicopter.

'*Mon Dieu!* Jean-Paul, we've run out of garlic, just hang on a moment while I get the chopper out and buzz down to the corner shop.'

Alfred Wills would be pleased to see us enjoy ourselves, although the helicopter might surprise him. Wills was the Englishman who built the Refuge and who also founded the Alpine Club. In his day the Refuge was a useful base-camp for assaults on the surrounding mountains and, of course, the provisions were brought up by packhorses.

There may be no such thing as a free lunch, but I paid twice for that meal. I paid the second price in muscular pain as I made the one thousand feet climb up to the next col. By now, I was well above the tree line so the views were distant and panoramic. A fine lake, Lac Anterne came into view at the foot of the escarpment of the Rochers de Fiz making it appear all the more like a giant castle, now complete with its moat. For the second time, I caught up with the Cheshire Chavs who were making good progress, steaming up a steep incline at an impressive rate. Their progress was yet another silent rebuke to my prejudices. Never again would I judge a Chav by her bling.

I had been looking forward all day to reaching the ridge at the Col D'Anterne. By my reckoning, Madame Mont Blanc would be able to hide no more and I would have a view over the next ridge of Mont Brevant to the very tops of Mont Blanc herself. I was disappointed. I have absolutely no idea whether there is such a view – it was far too misty to see the next ridge let alone the one after that.

From the col it was but a short descent to the Refuge de Moede. Despite my nine-hour day, now there was a beer in prospect, I ran down the 700 foot descent in my steady Kinabalu trot. And what a beer it turned out to be. Refuge de Moede specialised in green ale – a refreshing brew, in spite of all appearances to the contrary, with a flavour somewhere between Danish lager and English ginger beer. Eventually we made quite a party, three Swiss I had met up at the misty col, the Scottish Saints, the Cheshire Chavs and myself. We all drank several glasses of green beer without apparent harm or any noticeable change of complexion. As far as I can remember.

Although I had realised the folly of stereotyping such free spirits as the Cheshire Chavs, I was surprised and not a little impressed to learn that at home they grew grapes and made their own wine. I dreamed of planting extensive vineyards on south-facing slopes besides the Tees, and of copious vats of my own private wine from my two-acre domain which I would bottle as Chateau d'Hartlepool Superieur. The green beer must have got to me.

The three German-speaking Swiss, Anna, Hans and Theo, worked for a large international company based in Geneva and they were having a few days respite from their high-powered careers in not-stop, high-speed globalisation. These were bright-eyed young high-fliers with eager smiling faces. They were the kind of people I find interesting to talk to in a bar or on a long train journey, but a little too earnest to invite home to dinner. Of course, Murphy's Law ensured that when supper was served I found myself seated next to them. We were served Fondue Savoyard which, as far as I can tell, was a base of cheese flavoured with cheese; a hint of garlic or a dash of kirsch would not have gone amiss. I had my own table heater, an armoury of long-pronged forks, a big basket full of chunks of bread and a saucepan of hot, semi-molten cheese. I spent the next hour dealing with this apparatus under instruction, delivered with Teutonic precision, of my Swiss friends who, needless to say, were Gold Medallists in fondue-eating.

'You must always the cheese with your left hand stir. The bread with the right hand into the cheese is put.'

I obediently stirred the saucepan with a fork in my left hand, while my right hand speared a piece of bread, dipped it into the cheese-melt, performed a deft, figure-of-eight twist, withdrew the bread with its dripping coating, revolved it several times to discourage molten cheese from dropping onto my shirt-front, finally transferring the steaming glob to my mouth. By the end of it, I was exhausted. But I was rejuvenated by the respectful smiles on the three faces; I had clearly gained entry, at some apprentice rank, into a highly important and secret Swiss brotherhood of fondue-eaters.

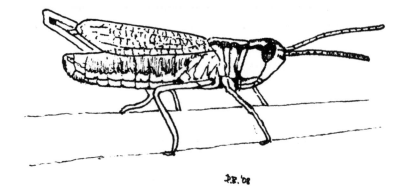

P.E. '08

Chapter Six

The Temptress Laid Bare

The closer I got to her the more she covered herself; Madame Mont Blanc was not making it easy for me on this trip. This was the day when I would be close enough to touch her but I realised I would be very lucky just to see her. The morning was cold and misty and everything was damp to the touch. The conditions were miserable but there was the cheering thought of a downhill start; a comfortable walk twelve hundred feet down to the Pont d'Arleve. Here the footpath crosses the River Diosaz as it cut its way aggressively and directly down the mountain, through a series of dramatic gorges. The stream was a pussycat at this time of year but at snow-melt it becomes a roaring tiger of a torrent taking everything before it. The bridge was such a light structure that it seemed inevitable the tiger would smash and twist it beyond use come next Spring. Then I noticed that the fixings were temporary. Apparently, when the Refuge Warden comes down the mountain at the end of summer he lifts the bridge and puts it safely to one side until the beginning of the next summer.

The downhill advantage was short-lived; from the bridge the path tackles Mont Brevant, which demands a steady climb of some three-and-a-half hours. I was in the midst of scenery as beautiful as any in the whole of Europe only for the clouds to blindfold me. I had climbed Mont Brevant some years earlier, when I had made the Tour of Mont Blanc with some friends, and I still carried vivid memories. I remembered this particular mountainside covered with flowers of every hue. I recalled the most spectacular views of Mont Blanc just across the valley, with its guardian pinnacles and its supporting glaciers sparkling, seemingly close enough to touch. I was mouthing vulgar curses against the mist when I was undeservedly compensated. A doe chamois hopped out onto the path not twenty feet in front of me; something she certainly would not have done in clear visibility. She was so close that I could see the condensed breath in her nostrils and the water droplets on her longer fur. For her part, she took an unhurried and inquisitive look at me with deep brown, alluring eyes; she bowed her head in dignified, almost regal, acknowledgement of my presence and then, effortlessly, she jumped. She jumped two feet into the air with her hooves daintily curved beneath her. Her elegant vertical take-off magically transferred into forward motion in mid-air, then she was off down the hill and into the mist. It was the most graceful sight that I have ever had the good fortune to see.

By noon, the stark angularities of the cable-car station at Mont Brevant loomed out of the mist. The word Brevant derives from the local vernacular for 'steep', and it is an understatement. There was nothing in view that was not steep. Standing on the large metal balcony that cantilevers out from a sheer rock face, I looked for Mont Blanc, but I looked in vain. I have photographs of me and my friends from my previous visit, on that very balcony. We are laughing in the sunshine as we admire the views of the glaciers across the valley. In the photographs Mont Blanc looks close enough for a long arm to reach out and touch.

In that cold, damp atmosphere, I wondered how long I would have to wait for those fantastic views to open up before me. Should I stay or should I go? I got no help from the Scottish Saints; they were firmly ensconced in the café for the rest of the day. This might have been because of the hard and long climb up from Pont d'Arleve, but more likely it was due to the presence of a lively group of French girls laughing in the corner.

The cloud showed not the slightest sign of lifting so I wished good-luck to my Scottish friends and took the cable car down to Chamonix. Purists on the GR5 would never dream of using a cable-car. Certainly not – they would walk down the long shoulder of the Grand Belcon to the valley at Les Hooches. The fact that I had walked it before did not really ease my conscience.

Safe and secure in the cable car station, the idea of descending in a little box hanging by a thread had seemed fairly innocuous. Once aboard, a sudden lurch quickly shattered my serenity. The sickening, downward drop and loud, mechanical clang terrified me. My pulse rate tripled and my heart was in my mouth. Then the jerks gave way to more genteel sways and slowly my heart fell back into place. All was quiet and peaceful. It was as if I had returned to the womb. I was warm, absolutely isolated and insulated from the rest of the world, swaying gently in total silence in almost zero visibility. If only it had lasted. One moment cocooned, the next launched into the world and brought face to face with the horrors of real life. Here I was, in a box the size of a coffin, dangling from miniscule metal rod which in its turn was attached to a cable by a bootlace. This thread swooped from pylon to pylon down the mountain. But why were the pylons so far apart? Why were they so flimsy, built with such an obvious eye to economics rather than to strength? I closed my eyes struggled for self-control. I told myself that the engineer had designed the whole thing with a safety factor of about ten! Then I opened my eyes and worried that he could so easily have misplaced a decimal point.

It did not bear thinking about, so I concentrated on the view. Here at last was the fabled, north side of Mont Blanc just in front of me. Every small detail of its needles, its cliff faces and glaciers came intermittently into view as the patchy cloud swirled by. Below, the houses and streets of Chamonix looked so tiny, as if I was looking down on an Ordnance Survey map. It was a heart-stopping descent, and the adrenalin flowed from the moment of my birth from the clouds to the time of my safe delivery at Chamonix station. Next time, I think I'll walk.

It was Sunday morning and Chamonix was in festival. Cheering crowds lined the streets, the sun was shining and the lower slopes of Mont Blanc were suddenly standing dramatically clear. Here was recognition at last. The good citizens obviously had news of my imminent arrival and were making appropriate arrangements to greet me with the honour I deserved. Alas, the crowds were cheering mountain-runners coming from the opposite direction after the non-stop, 150-kilometre Tour de Mont Blanc race. That any mortal can run, more or less non-stop, for 150 kilometres I find barely credible; that anybody can run that distance around Mont Blanc is totally beyond my powers of comprehension.

Of all athletic competitions, this surely takes the human body closest to the very limit of endurance. I have walked the Tour de Mont Blanc and I consider myself a pretty fine fellow for that. I have dined out on the story for years. I tell everyone how hard it was. After all, there are six passes to be conquered each requiring several thousand feet of climbing. With every up there is a down – six descents which may give some relief to the lungs but which wreak havoc on all the leg joints. Simply to have completed that circuit is quite a feather in my cap where I come from. Yet it took me six days. I only walked in daylight when I could see where I was going, I had six nights of good sleep, six slap-up dinners and probably six hundred and sixty-six water breaks. My respect for these runners knows no bounds. I could only stand in that sunlit square, still wobbling from my nerve-wracking descent, and join the rest of the appreciative crowd in loud applause. Stephentophe Jaquerod is the Olympian superhero who came home first in the unbelievable time of 21 hours, 11 minutes and 7 seconds. How he deserved the applause, but I will have to find a new after-dinner story.

A long, leisurely lunch in that festive atmosphere put paid to any lingering thoughts of walking further that day. I sat there in the afternoon sun with my attention divided between the now close-up wonders of the great mass of Mont Blanc and the cheerful holiday crowds. Possibly under the influence of a little alcohol, the two fused in my mind and I had a vision of Nero fiddling while Rome burned. The streets were throbbing with happy, smiling people while just above them disaster loomed. There are millions, if not trillions of tons of ice and rock hanging over Chamonix and bearing down inexorably upon the town. It may not set off the speed cameras, but that ice will arrive at Chamonix sooner or later. The Bossons Glacier is many square miles in area and thousands of feet in depth. It is the biggest ice cascade in Europe. It reminded me of a skeletal hand, icy-fingered, knuckled and gnarled, reaching down the gullies towards the valley and the town, scratching away and remorselessly grinding to dust any rocks or trees in its path. It is creeping towards Chamonix at the rate of ten metres per year. Of all the towns in the world, Chamonix must be the most enthusiastic about the advent of global warming. With luck, those icy fingers will melt on the very outskirts of the town.

From time to time, Bossons yields grizzly reminders of the human tragedies it has witnessed, if not caused. The Hamel Group fell on an expedition to the summit in 1820 and forty years later the glacier disgorged their refrigerated remains some four kilometres away. In 1978, the glacier discharged a postbag from the Indian aeroplane, the Malabar Princess, which had crashed near the summit in 1953. There are undoubtedly more artefacts and bodies trapped and preserved in that bumper deep-freeze.

A surprise arrival shook me out of my reverie. Stephen was casually strolling down the street. After our brief encounter in Novel, I expected never to see him again. Here he was, decked out in designer jeans, expensive shades and extravagant trainers. This was no walker relaxing; this was a dude on the prowl.

We had a beer together while he described his whole career as a walker; a distinguished record of achievement over two whole days that had taken him all the way from the lows of St Gingolph to the heights of Abondance. Evidently, the analytical intelligence of the computer programmer had convinced him to give up walking and take to the bus. He had a way with words, did Stephen. 'The GR5's too effing 'ard.'

I suffered only the slightest twinge of guilt when I caught the bus to Les Hooches. There, another cable-car took me up to a hotel. Hotel Le Prarion provides as fine a panorama as any hotel in Europe. On a clear day there is unrestricted sight of the whole of the south side of Mont Blanc while in the other direction, La Chaine des Arabis forms a dramatic horizon. At last I had the temptress unashamedly revealed before me in all her beauty. Without doubt this is the Empress of the Mountains of Europe. As she stands high, gathering her screes, cliffs and glaciers around her like so many petticoats, she seems to be floating over the Chamonix valley. The huge white mound of the Dome de Gouter swells up from the petticoats, holding the eye like a voluptuous buttock.

In the hotel I indulged in the luxury of a bath. Generally in rural France, hotels do not do baths. In the small-town, two-star hotels that I love so dearly good plumbing is generally not a feature. The standard is a shower cubicle with doors that do not quite close and a flexible hose that invariably leaks. If there is a bath, it is usually too small for me. I have the choice of covering my legs so that my calf muscles can relax while my body gets cold, or lying flat to keep my stomach warm while my knees freeze. The Hotel Le Prarion does baths. I had a cavernous Victorian tomb of a bath, submerged to the chin in very hot water.

Sundown at Le Prarion is an exceptional event. The sun was behind me as it set, creating on Mont Blanc a myriad of fascinating lighting effects playing on the face of the mountain; as it sank behind La Chaine des Arabis those mountains were silhouetted and all the colour play was in the sky. On that fantastic evening it was hard to believe that I was the only diner in that stunning, panoramic room. Any other time, I would have been disgruntled at having to eat alone but on this particular occasion I was delighted; I was far too pre-occupied to have time for other people. I spent the whole time grabbing a mouthful to eat, dashing with my camera to one side of the room, swallowing another mouthful with perhaps a quick swig and then dashing to the other side for another photograph.

The Mont Blanc view held more detail. Initially, light cloud drifted around the middle heights of the mountain, but this slowly cleared to reveal the cliffs of La Tête Rousse with its tiny Refuge perched on top. I recalled that when I climbed Mont Blanc I had scrambled up that almost-vertical cliff and had snatched a very short night's sleep in that self-same Refuge. Unlike this hotel, the place had been so crowded that people were sleeping on stair landings. Everyone left in darkness in the early hours with the intention of reaching the summit by sunrise, wearing torches on their foreheads to light their way. I was one of the last to leave the Refuge in the cold, starlit wee hours. A line of walkers straggled ahead, picked out by their headlights, snaking upwards. As they got further away their, lights got smaller and higher until, in the end, they were indistinguishable from the stars. It felt as if I was following a starlit trail to heaven. Sitting in the dining room with those memories, I picked out the route we must have followed over the Dome du Gouter to the top. The Dome was pure, sparkling white in the full sun but in the changing light it turned through subtle tones of pink before slowly darkening to mauves. The blue of the sky seemed to get paler before changing through deep marine blues to the mauves of the mountain as the night finally overcame all light.

By contrast, from the other side of the room, La Chaine des Arabis seemed to be on fire. The mountains, stark, jagged and black were the coals. The sky behind was aflame with brilliant, flickering gold with flashes of blue slowly turning to deep reds. And I had it all to myself. To crown my smug satisfaction, Mont Brevant had remained wrapped in cloud all day, though I doubt that the Scottish Saints and the French girls had even noticed.

Chapter Seven

'Und now, my brassière I take away'

Snaking across the mountain pastures just below Le Prarion and small enough to be almost unnoticeable is a narrow-gauge track. It is nearly overgrown and easily overlooked today but it still represents a triumph for the alpine engineers who built it in 1902. This is the famous Mont Blanc tramway built to take tourists from the comforts of the valley at Saint-Gervaise to the wilds of the Nid d'Aigle, the Eagle's Nest, high up amongst the towers and pinnacles flanking the Mont Blanc summit. The engineer in me was interested. The tram has a rack device, not dissimilar to the cogs and chain of a bicycle, so that it can slowly but surely climb gradients as severe as one in four. For more than a hundred years the train has taken many tens of thousands of people to the dizzy heights of the Mont Blanc Massif. People who, but for the skill and enterprise of those engineers, would never have left the security of the valley and would certainly never have experienced the joy of being among the peaks of very high mountains.

The valley of the Bon Nant River is home to a string of small traditional alpine villages with exotic-sounding names:

Bionnassay, la Gruvaz, le Quy. As I walked from one pearl to the next I kept pinching myself. Had I passed through a time-warp? The hamlets seem almost unchanged from the agricultural workshops they were one hundred years ago. The buildings are predominantly built of wood, are functional and unpainted, with low pitches to the roofs. These sweeping roofs have large overhangs to cope with the heavy snows of winter. Surrounded by a landscape of traditional farm-buildings, gentle gradients, mixed woodlands against a backdrop of mountains under that clear blue sky, I was walking in heaven.

In this contented state of mind, I found it hard to imagine that this valley was once the scene of a horrendous natural disaster which killed over 200 people in one savage night. At the head of the Bionassay Valley lies the Tête Rousse glacier, a small chunk of ice by the standards of these parts. In 1892, the glacier began to melt internally for reasons not fully understood to this day. Eventually the concentrated weight of the water in the centre burst the bubble of the remaining ice which was forming the skin of the glacier. One night in July, thousands of tons of water and ice crashed down the valley smashing to smithereens anything and everything that stood before it. The huge wave entirely swept away the hamlets of Bionnassay and Bionnay and rushed on. Confined and strengthened by the narrow defile of the valley, the force blasted into the Thermal Baths of Saint-Gervaise instantly killing 150 people. The water rush finally reached the plains of the Arve where it spread out and dissipated, in the process discharging a thick layer of mud, rock and human debris.

I stood in that beautiful, tranquil alpine scene, overwhelmed by images of the horror of the calamity. Perhaps, after all, I should go back and parade down Chamonix High Street with a placard reading, 'The End is Nigh – Remember Bionnassay!' Then again, perhaps it would be less daft to walk on to Les Contamines and have a stiff brandy.

On the way, I tripped from nineteenth century tragedy into twenty-first century farce. Just below Bionnassay I was forced off a narrow cart track by a convoy of at least twenty four-by-four vehicles. With gross, chromium-plated cow-catchers to the front, fat tyres spinning from the insensitive clutch-control of a city driver, hugely over-powered engines over-revving, monstrous chrome twin exhausts emitting clouds of noxious, black smoke, the convoy churned its way nose-to-tail along the track. Each driver had an exhilarating view of the mud-spewing rear-end of the vehicle in front. There must be a place for four-by-fours in this world of ours; there must be people who buy them for eminently practical and justifiable reasons. Australian sheep farmers and Arizonan cattle magnates surely find them a godsend. There is something wrong when people, having bought the ghastly gas-guzzlers, need to join guided, day-trip convoys into the wilderness just for the sake of justifying their purchase, like overgrown boys in the park still holding nanny's hand. And it was all so unnecessary. On foot and unaccompanied, I would get further and I would see and hear far more that day than they would from their personalised number-plated, climate-killing carbon-emitters. I would leave nothing but footprints; they would see and hear practically nothing and, in the process, would pollute the atmosphere and churn up tracks to make them impassable. I stood aside to let them pass with all their noise and fumes, clart and spatter.

I had stopped fuming by the time I reached Les Contamines-Montjoie in perfect time for morning coffee. Like Samoens and Chamonix, Les Contamines was cheerful, colourful and welcoming. Its name derives apparently from an ancient word for a piece of land reserved for the Lord of the Manor and exempt from tax. I am all in favour of these ancient traditions and argue for their preservation. Sad to say, the restaurateurs of Les Contamines do not share my views – there was no suggestion of tax-relief on the bill for my coffee.

England were playing Australia in the fourth Test and I toyed with the idea of persuading the barman to flick through his television channels to see if we could get the score, but I remembered that the French don't do cricket any more than they do baths. They have no word for it, let alone a TV channel. If I wanted him to find a UK channel, I would have to mime, which would involve an ostentatious charge down the road with my arms swinging wildly. They were not likely to take kindly to my bowling a yorker in a crowded High Street. If I was going to keep a low profile, I had to forget the cricket.

I nearly succumbed to the temptation to linger and stretch the coffee-break to lunchtime, but the cool, calm and collected me took control and voted for the mountains. As there were two or three days of wilderness walking ahead I stocked up with some basic provisions. I try never to be without a tin of sardines, some local cheese and some dried fruit in my pack. Whenever I see a soft, ripe Canteloupe melon on display my iron will melts, my resolute discipline over pack-weight crumbles and I surrender to temptation. I reckoned the sardines would see me through any twenty-four hour emergency; with the melon I could party in the meantime.

I suffered a knock to the ego leaving the town. I lost my way trying to thread through the modern ski-resort development on the outskirts. Hopefully nobody was watching. It can be easier to navigate across snow-covered moors in the mist than to find your way through a maze of modern streets. The answer is to keep it simple. I knew I had merely to find and follow the river and eventually the right path would unfold before me. It did, of course, and at length I was walking beside the river on an ancient packhorse route threading through the forest southwards into the wilds.

I thought I had left all traces of civilisation behind me and that I was having a vision. There, in a clearing across the river, was a beautiful church. The Church of Notre Dame of the Gorges is pure baroque and today its white-rendered walls sparkled brilliantly in the sunshine. Why was a church of such distinctive charm and vitality built here so remote from any population? Never walk past an unanswered question, is my motto. Like a magnet the mystery lured me across the bridge for a closer inspection. An engraved plaque high up on the front façade informed the visitor (providing he could read Latin) that 'the foundations of the church rest on the mountain Saints'. That explained it. This is the Chapel of the Crossing. Who, in an age of faith, was going to risk the hazards of the alpine passes ahead without a last-minute prayer and a donation? Who, having successfully negotiated those hazards, was not going to stop on returning and make a prayer and a gift of thanks? Upon reflection, this remote spot is an entirely appropriate place for a church. Lord Byron and Victor Hugo presumably both thought so when they signed the Visitor's Book years ago.

I read of a charming folk tale associated with the Chapel. If my translation of the French can be trusted, it goes something like this. A pot-bellied man and his flat-chested wife went and prayed to Our Lady of the Gorges for some relief from the trials and tribulations of their earthly toil. Our Lady took pity on them and organized a supernatural transplant, transferring 'a layer of corpulence' from the one to the other. Their prayers answered, the couple went happily on their way; he with a six-pack of a stomach and she amply padded where required. I think I might set up an agency. I can think of coach-loads of couples who would benefit considerably from a chat with Our Lady of the Gorges.

While I did not kneel and pray for a safe journey ahead, I did walk on undoubtedly moved by the inspirational beauty of the building created by those men of faith. This was no modern footpath bulldozed out to encourage the new walking-tourism. I was on a very ancient track, the strategic route from the Middle Rhone Valley in France to the Aosta Valley in Italy. Roman Legions certainly marched this way and, near the chapel, there is a Roman bridge to prove it. Doubtless men had walked this very path millennia before that. I was walking shoulder to shoulder with the ghosts of pilgrims, merchants, soldiers and rogues of seven thousand years of history.

A steep climb through the forest eventually brought me to a pastured valley, bordered with stands of high conifers on either side. Almost on cue, in this archetypal alpine scene, a black woodpecker flew across my path. With its distinctive scarlet crest it must have been a male, since the females are more discreet with only a little red at the nape of the neck. The trees in the distance were probably Norway spruces, a favourite in the black woodpecker diet, which they have followed in their recent southwards colonisation.

Refreshment stops conveniently and frequently punctuated the walk on this section. After my coffee at Les Contamines, I enjoyed a little aperitif in the garden of Refuge Nant Borrant before lunching at Refuge la Balme. The lunch was special; a thin slice of rare steak sprinkled with garlic, and a well-dressed salad. As I ate, warmed by the sun beneath the high ridge de Fours, in an amphitheatre of mountains, I realised I was as close as I am ever likely to get, on this earth or the next, to eating the food of the Gods in the Palace of the Gods. I can well understand why many people make a day-trip of walking from Les Contamines to La Balme, enjoying a fine lunch in the spectacular landscape and walking back again. It is a walking-gourmet's ideal day, particularly with a black woodpecker for a bonus.

Col de Bonhomme is a remote, high pass. Happily for the geriatric climber, the path rises like a giant's staircase. I made a series of short, steep and hard hill climbs to gain intermediate short walks on approximately horizontal sections. Here my pulse rate could come down, my breathing patterns recover and my throbbing heart could begin to hope it might live for another hour. The daily struggle up the mountainside was still proving tough although, of course, that was in no way related to that second glass of wine I had enjoyed at lunch. I fell in with an Australian couple, on holiday from Sydney, and I suddenly remembered again that this was the fourth day of the Fourth Test between England and Australia. I asked if they had news of the score.

In deadpan, Sydney-speak they grunted, 'You won by three wickets.'

The well-mannered Englishman buried deep inside me responded politely,

'How nice! That is a surprise.'

I waited for a congratulatory, 'Good on yer, yer Pommie bastard,' but I waited in vain.

To hear that England has beaten Australia is always sweet news. To hear it from an Australian was pure honeyed ambrosia. I purred up the remainder of that mountain powered by pride, heartlessly leaving the two dispirited Aussies trudging behind, carrying their rucksacks and tattered dreams. On the way is a pillar-shaped rock which, legend has it, marks the graves of an English lady and her servant who died in a terrible blizzard. The folklore advises the traveller to add a stone to the natural cairn as a mark of respect to the lady and as thanks for good fortune. Superstitious twaddle – this is the age of reason. But nobody was looking, so I carefully laid two rocks; one in memory of the English lady and one for the victorious cricket team.

A group of Dutch walkers cheered me up the last steep slope to the Col du Bonhomme. After expressions of mutual disappointment at the lack of a bar in the vicinity we celebrated our ascent with a sacrificial feast of some of their oranges and all of my juicy Canteloupe melon – sacrificial not in the sense that we were appeasing the Gods but rather that I gave away most of the mouth-watering melon that I had lugged all the way up that mountain. I wanted to make sure that they did not eat it all.

'Leave some for me,' I said, 'that is all that stands between me and starvation.'

One of the women took a slow, deliberate look at my profile and in perfect English told me.

'There is a good six months between you and starvation.'

Refreshed, we walked together the short distance to the more famous Col de la Croix du Bonhomme. Here the challenges unfolded before me. To the south-west the mountains of Tarentaise glinted gold in the light of the lowering sun. To the south-east lay the region of Beaufortain, its mountains dark and purple in silhouette. Overwhelmed by the beauty of the view, it struck me how gently curved and feminine mountains look when viewed from the tops; how craggy, aggressive and masculine they look when viewed from below.

Of more immediate interest to me, and not a hundred yards ahead, was the Refuge. After ten hours walking, an oasis in the desert could not have presented a more welcome sight than the Refuge de la Col de la Croix du Bonhomme. The long-winded name is perhaps appropriate for a Refuge which serves walkers on several routes, including my present task-master, the GR5, and my old friend, the Tour de Mont Blanc. The Refuge was crowded with walkers of all nationalities. I shared a bunk room with seven generously endowed German Brunhildes and two strapping young Frenchmen.

The meal was another communal, international affair. I shared the tureens on my table with two long-legged, extremely energetic Dutchmen, the Australian couple (apparently recovered from their cricket trauma) and a young billy-cooing couple from Paris.

The appearance of a small herd of chamois moving along the nearby ridge, silhouetted in the setting sun, interrupted the soup course. They obviously keep well away from the footpaths and stay on the very high ground during the day, moving more freely at dusk and dawn. Often, when walking high up in the Alps, the valleys sweep up in swathes of impassable rocky screes defending the high pastures. The distant tinkle of a falling stone is a signal to stop and look up. There they are, picking their way along the grassland at the very top of the thousand-foot scree slope; a small family of chamois. Invariably a stag leads the way, always alert, dignified and sedate. Four or five females, dainty, delicate and deliberate, follow. Around them, half a dozen calves skitter and skittle with the boundless energy of the young, scattering the stones.

The chamois were quickly forgotten when a steaming Reblochonade was laid before us in a veritable cauldron, containing ham and bacon in chunky abundance in a base of bread and the ubiquitous cheese – the Savoyards certainly like their cheese. Reblochon cheese, like Abondance, is a cheese with a history. Once upon a time, or so the story goes, the farmers were forced to pay their landlords an additional rent which was in proportion to the milk production of their cows. When the fee was about to be collected, the farmers artfully reduced the milk production. When the agent had gone, with much glee and chortling, they had a second, furtive milking, known in the local vernacular as the *reblochi*. The whiff of Revolution adds an extra tang to a cheese.

The Refuge de la Croix du Bonhomme maintains one of the great traditions of the alpine Refuge. Once we had eaten and cleared the tables, the entertainment began. The family who run the Refuge had been busy cooking and serving supper and had yet to do the washing-up, but they still managed to put on a concert. Philippe started with a serenade on his violin. Francois bundled him off stage to perform a trombone solo. Papa came on with his guitar. Susanne tried to play her recorder. Mama sang. The family fell over themselves to entertain, sometimes solo, sometimes ensemble and, quite often, in tune. Father and sons sported dreadlocks and their faces were creased with laughter lines. With their puffing red cheeks and bulbous noses they needed no make-up to look like circus clowns. This was a family born to entertain, and they left a contented audience of walkers to find their way to bed.

It will be some time before I am able to erase from my memory the full horror of that night. In our cosmopolitan mixed dormitory were seven mature German Fraus, and it was like being trapped in a Wagnerian opera.

The two Frenchmen and I, men who had fearlessly trekked the mountains of the world, sat on our bunks and fiddled around taking off our socks and looking for our night clothes with focussed concentration. We were more than a little overwhelmed by the seven, vociferously lusty, busty beauties. Brunhilde on the bunk opposite fixed me with a gimlet gaze as she took off her shirt, and wallowed towards me with more rolling curves, more rippling bulges and more straining guy-ropes than a galleon in full sail. No more than three feet away she stopped, braced her legs and reached behind her to the small of her back. 'Und now', she said, making sure she had our complete attention, 'Und now, my brassiere I take away.' The three of us shot into our sleeping bags, like rabbits bolting down a burrow. Fully-clothed, one sock off and the other on, I hid there all night, not daring to take a peek until morning, when I was sure that all seven had upped and left. Only then did my two fearless French comrades-in-arms emerge from their sleeping bags.

I have spent many a night in mixed dormitories without any similar confrontation. Normally, people move off quietly and change in their own shower-rooms. Everyone behaves demurely and excessively politely and there is no embarrassment. Thinking of the number of Refuges on the footpath network across France there must, on any one night be one stunningly attractive, young female flitting across the dormitory in something silky and flimsy, but I have never seen her. I suppose I shall just have to keep on walking.

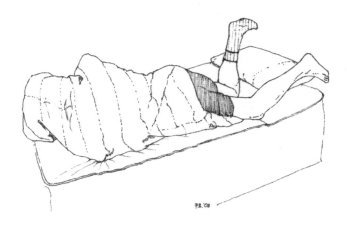

Chapter Eight

Sorry, France is Closed

The next day it was like walking along the back of a giant, fossilised mountainosaurus. The GR5 led out of the Refuge along a very sharp ridge where, at times, the path was no more than a narrow ledge. On my right was a rock-slope falling steeply all the way to a mortuary of rocks. On my left was a slightly less daunting prospect, falling only as far as the accident ward of broken legs. Once I had pictured the bloody meat ball that would be me if I slipped in either direction, I walked with the greatest care, wishing I had Sherpa Tensing and a rope. When I managed to concentrate my mind on the mountains around rather than on the rocks below, I felt physically and spiritually on top of the world.

The long-limbed Dutch couple had tried to convince me the previous night that the military had cut this ridge-path for their own purposes. The path is so narrow that I found that hard to believe. It never was wide enough for a cart or a gun-carriage, although pack-horses might have got across with a fatality rate of about one in five. Walking the ridge early in the morning with the angled sun lending perspective and emphasis to peaks, ridges and valleys in all directions it was hard to imagine the need for soldiers up here. The petty squabbles of men seemed insignificant and unnecessary in this world of mammoth mountains.

Far below, I could just make out some walkers slowly threading their way up towards me. There is always deep satisfaction, even *schadenfreude*, in storming down a hill with a long stride and shouting an excessively cheerful '*Bonjour*' to walkers painfully picking their way up, knowing they can hardly find the breath to grunt a reply. At the time, I quite forget that it will soon be my turn to crawl up a hill while some loose-limbed, obnoxiously cheerful idiot bounds down.

Everything that morning was a work of art that pleased the eye. There were woodlands and pastures close at hand; glaciers, lakes and waterfalls in the distance; mountains as a backdrop. All were in perfect harmony, making ideal compositions wherever I looked. I cannot conceive in my mind a paradise more beautiful; even though I was walking away from the greatest of masterpieces.

I kept glancing behind me to say my last farewells to my mixed metaphor. Over the past seven days, the enormous bulk of Mont Blanc had dominated the route. During most of that time, particularly from a distance, I had seen the mountain as a temptress luring me on with the occasional bare shoulder before slipping behind a screen of cloud, then, finally exposing that rounded white buttock of the Dome de Gouter. At times, particularly when close and sitting under those frightening walls of ice in Chamonix, I had imagined the mountain as a sinister skeleton. Now, at this distance, Mont Blanc shrugged off all its metaphorical guises and simply became the biggest, the most beautiful, the most magnificent mountain in all Europe.

Jewels were scattered in my path. Small clumps of gentians with purple-blue flowers sparkled in the breeze, as if so many sapphires had been strewn at my feet. Below me, Lac de Roseland shimmered like a polished emerald, dazzling and exotic. The beauty all around lulled me into euphoria. A high, castellated wall of sheer mountain formed the horizon to the south. So what? It was two or three hours walking ahead. At that distance it did not seem necessary, let alone possible, to have to climb over that wall. Surely there was a pass, a breach in the wall, hidden by a fold in the mountains.

I was sublimely happy. For the next two or three hours I walked in blissful, self-deluding ignorance focussing on my immediate surroundings, rather than on mountain walls ahead. A couple of marmots popped up on sentry-go on a scatter of rocks beside the path. They seemed unafraid and allowed me to get quite close. Why should a marmot worry about me when it has evolved a unique and highly successful survival strategy? It tastes foul. It tastes so absolutely awful that no other creature can bear to eat it. I have only ever met one Frenchman who confessed to eating marmot, and he did so with a slightly shame-faced air. You have to be desperate to eat marmot, and he confessed that his grandparents had been poor shepherds who apparently ate marmot when there was nothing else. Even the French, who can make something appetising out of snails and frogs, are defeated by marmot. The foul-tasting meat lies beneath a layer of even nastier-tasting, stinking fat. The shepherds would leave the creature soaking in water for days on end before stripping away the fat and cooking the meat.

It is lucky for marmots that they taste and smell so disgusting since they are not smart at evading danger. At the first hint of trouble – a walker, say, dislodging a stone some yards away – the marmot, until then hidden and safely camouflaged among the rocks, catches your attention by standing upright on its hind legs and waving its head in the air. Eventually it runs off, but, to make absolutely sure that no one loses sight of it, it waves its tail in the air like a child running through the long grass with a balloon on a string. Then, in case you weren't concentrating, it pops up onto its hind legs again to see if you are still following. Finally it drops into its hole.

Gradually the climb became steeper. The chances of finding hidden folds in the wall ahead became less and less likely. I could avoid the horrible reality no longer; the path must go straight over the top. By the time that unwelcome truth had struck home I had little alternative but to grit my teeth, swear profusely and stagger on. As I trudged slowly upwards, my passion for the mountains began to wane.

I hate climbing mountains.

'What the hell am I doing here?' I asked myself.

If Confucius had been a mountain-climber he would undoubtedly have said: 'Do not think of the future unless you can see it below you!'

I resorted to moronic mantras.

'Get to that blue rock. Get to that blue rock. Get to that blue rock.'

Then I ring the changes.

'Get to that bend. Get to that bend. Get to that bend.'

Then suddenly it is all over and I am reborn. I have reached the top and that moment of magical reincarnation obliterates all my doubts. The pain, the panting, the pulse rates are instantly forgotten in the euphoria of the achievement, and by the wonder and the sheer joy of seeming to be literally on top of the world.

I love climbing mountains.

As the curtain rises on the next backdrop, the spirit stirs with the adrenalin of success, of being in an exclusive place reached only by blood, sweat and tears and of being rewarded by dramatic vistas in all directions. I always look back to seek out the ridges and mountains that I climbed yesterday or the day before and I remember the exhilaration and the beauty of those pinnacles, forgetting the price paid to reach them. Then I look forward to the passes I will climb to-morrow and, with undiluted happiness, I say a prayer of thanks for being alive and for being here in this wilderness. My passion is rekindled. There is plenty of space for faith on the top of a mountain range.

Col de Bresson may have been demanding, but it was worth every effort. I sat on the border between Beaufortain and the Tarentais, and I enjoyed the panoramic view. My main interest lay to the south. I traced my approximate route down and across the Isère Valley, (where I would do my best to avoid ski-resorts) and up into the mountains of La Vanoise National Park. I could pick out, just east of south, the impressive bulk of Mount Pourri which I would get over in the coming days. For all I knew there were no other souls on the planet. I had not seen a soul since my '*Bonjours*' of five hours ago and I could see no sign of human activity, past or present. Feeling like a God on the Olympian heights I prepared myself a celebratory feast of all the cheese, sardines and bread that I had bought in Les Contamines yesterday. Later, I was to regret such indulgence.

I dawdled easily for an hour or so down from the Col to arrive at the Refuge du Balme, yet another cosy alpine chalet with its old-world charm just a wee bit marred by the helicopter wind-sock tied to a metal pole jutting out from the terrace. The sky was still blue, the sun was still warm and, more importantly, the route was downhill so I decided to continue for a couple of hours to the Auberge at Valezan. After a night in a bunk in a Refuge, any Auberge would be positively luxurious.

With the day's climb behind me, I still felt in good shape after some eight hours and was striding along no slower than at the beginning of the day. The Commune de Valezan laid on a special welcoming party to greet me after my two-day trek across the mountains. There were massed hordes of butterflies and restless cavalcades of grasshoppers. The butterflies were almost entirely varieties of small Silver-blues. Experts tell me it is difficult to identify them more precisely without a detailed examination of their genitalia – and I am not sure that is a suitable occupation for a gentleman. They gathered in their dozens at particularly delectable morsels on the path. How odd that such exquisite, delicate creatures as these should grow beautiful by feeding on sheep droppings.

75

What better example of the benefits of re-cycling than that set by these tiny iridescent Silver-blues. As I approached, the crowds scattered and dithered around my feet making me feel that swirling clouds of butterfly-confetti were blessing the very ground I trod. Among the myriads of Silver-blues was a scattering of Ringlets and Browns, some Pale Clouded Yellows and the occasional rich, bright yellow Brimstone. Kaleidoscopes of thousands of butterflies whirling, glittering and flashing their iridescence in the afternoon sun made an unforgettable sight. There was an explosion of colour as a Jersey Tiger Moth took off. Although it has a World War One bi-plane named after it, this bizarre creature is a large, diurnal moth that has the shape and arrogance of a World War Three stealth bomber. It is disdainful of camouflage. At rest, it is a delta-wing of jet-black with vivid white streaking; in flight it is a shooting fireball of reds and yellows.

Between the clouds of butterflies came the cavalcades of grasshoppers. These were no more evolutionarily advanced than those I had met at Anterne. With no apparent sense of purpose they jumped off in every direction, bounced, rolled over and jumped again in the opposite direction. With so many grasshoppers of so many colours jumping erratically in every direction, it was like walking through a field of Chinese crackers, with the sound off.

As if the celebration at my feet was not enough, the ever-thoughtful Commune had also arranged an aerial escort. A pair of Egyptian Vultures soared overhead. One hovered in the air currents almost stationary above me with only the slightest and infrequent ripple of adjustment to its wing tips or tail feathers to maintain its position. The other floated in majestic arcs until a squadron of four angry crows attacked, forcing it to make a tactical withdrawal and rejoin its mate. The two lazily circled each other, slowly getting higher and higher with the maximum of grace and the minimum of effort. They were light-years of evolution ahead of the grasshoppers.

Vultures may look elegant in the air, but on the ground they are the most revolting creatures. I have seen them hunting mercilessly in packs. Once I was on a ridge in the Pyrenees looking down on a pasture immediately below. A ewe and her new-born lamb had wandered a little way from the flock. Three vultures swooped down. The poor creature kept as close to its mother as it could, the ewe, determined to defend her offspring, bravely faced the stabbing, dagger-like beaks. But it was all too easy. The vultures placed themselves at the three points of a triangle around the sheep; the mother could only face off two at any one time. Inevitably, the third vulture darted in and pulled the lamb away. The three of them tore the creature to pieces in front of the helpless, hopeless ewe. I will carry to the grave pictures of that scene; stomach-churning proof that nature is red in tooth and claw.

On the approach into Valezan is a small roadside chapel; all the more picturesque because it is slowly, yet with dignity, sinking at an angle into the hillside. This simple structure hedges its bets with a dedication to three saints. Unfortunately, they had neglected to include the patron saint of foundations but my old friend St Roch was one of the three. Had he really been with me all the way from Neuteu?

By early evening, after some ten hours of steady walking, I arrived thirsty and hungry at Valezan, eager for the anticipated five-star delights of the Auberge. The place was closed; the doors were locked and there was no sign of life. I went round the village seeking information, hoping to find that this was some sort of joke and that the place would be doing a roaring trade in a few minutes time. No, apparently the hotel closed in September and the fact that it was August 30 was of little consequence to the owners. The next bed for hire was five miles along the route and, by that time, walking for two hours sounded just as unwelcome to me as walking for two days. I was miserably contemplating the prospects of dossing down in the bus shelter when along came the Auberge owner from a house along the street. He could give me a bed for the night, but he had no food and there was no shop in the village. How I regretted that indulgent lunch, especially the tinned sardines. Faced with a choice of walking for two hours to a meal and a bed, or sleeping on an empty stomach, I decided on the latter.

Monsieur proudly took me to the top floor of the Auberge which he had recently converted into a clean and comfortable Gite d'Etape. How lively it must be when full, but I was alone. I had a choice of thirty bunk beds in three rooms and of six swish shower cubicles. There was a kitchen equipped with every conceivable culinary necessity except food. Then, in a corner of a cupboard, I found a past-its-sell-by-date packet of spaghetti. Nothing else. I showered luxuriously, washed my clothes and dined alone on spaghetti, totally unflavoured and unsalted, washed down with carefully selected vintage tap-water in a plastic mug. I reminded myself that I had once lived for two days on puffed wheat with no milk or sugar. By comparison I was, after all, eating in five-star luxury tonight.

Chapter Nine

An Alpine Eisteddfod

Now that I had reached civilisation, or its near-equivalent at Valezan, I thought that I would treat myself to an easy day. After all, argued the devil-on-my-shoulder, I had hiked for two long days across the wilderness; I had climbed over the southern shoulder of Mont Blanc and then I had crossed the Massif de Beaufortain to arrive here in the Isère Valley.

'You deserve a rest,' whispered the devil.

'You are here to walk not to loll around,' replied my work-ethic conscience.

The lack of any morsel to trick my stomach into believing that it had breakfasted marred the pleasure of an undisturbed lie-in until 7.30. I could not find even a second-hand, green tea, grapefruit-flavoured tea-bag. If I wanted anything more than water I would have to walk on. Which was a pity. Valezan has an unusual, contrary-wise layout, with its main street following the line of the steepest slope of the hillside. Most villages contrive to have their main street on the level; Valezan, by contrast has level side streets. There were signs indicating a tour of the numerous architectural distinctions of this typical Tarentaise village, which half of me wanted to follow. But the other half was unable to enjoy architecture on an empty stomach. So I walked on in search of food.

The sun was shining as I walked down the valley past copses of hazel. This is a tree deeply rooted in our folklore. The Celts believed that eating the nuts gave wisdom. In medieval legend, Tristan lured Isolde away from her escort to a secret clearing in the forest by laying a trail of hazel branches with his name carved on them. The minstrels tell us that in the clearing they lay clasped in each others arms for two hours discussing politics. I know better. For a moment, I toyed with the idea of carving my name on a hazel branch and waiting to see what happened. But I was hungry and walked on to breakfast.

Dreaming of courtly love, or something similar, in no time at all I arrived at the small village of Bellentre. I made up for my enforced abstinence by gorging breakfast of hot, milky and very sweet coffee, croissants that had been baked on the premises that very hour, generously spread with butter and alternately crammed with home-made fig jam and apple-jelly. The devil-on-my-shoulder kicked the old work-ethic into touch. Today would be an easy day.

My strict dietary discipline of home had slowly collapsed under the onslaught of French culinary temptation. I do not diet to reduce my weight but more in the hope of changing my shape. If I live the indulgent life-style that I prefer I readily go to pot, literally. Doubtless, I was burning plenty of calories on my hikes but breakfasts like these were replacing those calories with a hefty dividend. I resolved to go on a diet; starting tomorrow. Meanwhile, I thought I might have the apple-jelly with that last croissant. I replenished my reserves with some bread and cheese, another juicy melon and, as ever, a tin of sardines. These were a special delicacy; sardines in a hot chilli-pepper sauce. Somewhere along the path I could treat myself to a gourmet's picnic.

The churches in the Tarentais are distinctive. It is as though a Russian Fairy-Princess has waved a magic wand and cast a spell on the churches built amongst the cow-byres of this remote French valley. Typically, a slender, white-stone square tower of elegant proportions supports an exotic, metal-clad superstructure of various geometrical shapes. A squat pyramid sits on top of the tower, with a large sphere spiked onto its apex. In turn, an elegant conical spire caps the sphere. Finally all is crowned with a cross pointing the way to heaven. The overall effect is inspiring and brings a touch of Eastern exoticism into villages where all the other buildings are simple; practical and efficient for their agricultural purposes. Bellentre has a fine example of the Tarentais church, although its superstructure has recently been re-clad in stainless-steel. The modernisation, of course, was not without tears. Was there ever a change, sacred or secular, that did not cause an argument between the modernisers and the traditionalists? The traditionalists of Bellentre wanted to keep their dilapidated, rusty, tin-plated old tower but were overruled by the young modernists. As a result, a fine church dominates Bellentre; a church with a silver tower that sparkles and shines in the sunlight. It is a thing of beauty and, this time, I am firmly on the side of the young ones.

While I was looking round the church a young priest hesitantly approached me, diffidently caught between an eagerness to please and an unwillingness to intrude. We had little common language, but he wanted to show me the monstrance on the altar table, a beautiful and ornate piece, with precious stones and silver figures and a curious provenance. Monsieur Cleaz, the son of a homeless peddler, born in this remote village in France, became a tradesman, married an heiress from Augsburg and ended up a merchant-by-appointment to Leopold, Archduke of Austria, King of Hungary and Bohemia. Rich and successful beyond his wildest dreams he remembered his humble roots. He donated the monstrance and inscribed it with the words, 'I, Jean-F Cleaz of Bellentre, bourgeois merchant of Augsburg, present this to my patron M. St Andre'.

The houses on one side of the main street in this village are huge – as big as a modern office block – and I wondered why. Again, the young priest came to my rescue and took me round one of the buildings. Once inside, I realised that these are not merely houses, they are farm-factories, with three uses provided for in one building. The ground floor, built into the slope of the land, is for the beasts and accessed from a courtyard which faces south is thus protected from the worst of the weather. A timber staircase climbs from the courtyard to a cantilevered gallery where the farmer and his family live. Above this is another floor, open on all sides with a strong timber framework supporting a massive, overhanging roof of giant stone slabs. This floor puzzled me. Eventually, with a great deal of sign language and not a little giggling, the priest got the message across. There is no autumn in this valley. The farmers must harvest the barley before the snows come, ripe or not. These spacious hay-lofts were vital for the survival of the agricultural community. Here the barley could ripen, undisturbed by snow or rain. The family would hardly need a fire in mid-winter with a herd of cows steaming below, thick stone walls all around with scarcely any windows and stacks of hay providing insulation above.

Poor these farmers may have been, but they still had to find something to do in the long winter's evenings. They developed wood-carving skills. On the first floor every available piece of timber is used to show off their craft. The hearts and roses carved all over the balustrades and doors not only look handsome but, according to local belief, they ward off evil spirits.

By these various unusual architectural features the Isère Valley has developed its own attractive identity. The delicate church spires and solid farmhouses are a statement of difference, a declaration of independence, which has deep roots in the history of the area. It was not always part of France. Several hundred years ago the Valley was part of an independent Dauphine region ruled from Grenoble by the Counts of Albon. Like Samoens, this is yet another example of a place-name derived from the old French heraldry, this time from the dolphin, or dauphin that dominated the coats of arms of the Counts. The family ruled the area, roughly equivalent to the modern departments of Isère, Drome and Hautes-Alpes, as their private fiefdom for nearly three hundred years. Until Count Humbert blew it all on unbridled religious extravagance. He financed several religious institutions, founded the University of Grenoble, enjoyed a costly lifestyle, went off on a Crusade to the Holy Land and came home bankrupt in 1349 to find his wife and son dead. Broken-hearted, he lost interest in this world and sold his fiefdom to the highest bidder. King Philipe VI of France made him an offer he could hardly refuse; 300,000 guilders in cash and a pension of 24,000 pounds a year. The only condition of the sale was that the heir to the French throne should henceforth be called 'Dauphin'.

The route out of Bellentre threatened to be boring since it follows the road. In the event, what I had expected to be a tedious slog of dusty road-marching, hustled by speeding cars, turned out to be a colourful and cheerful walk. Beside the road there were small meadows coloured pink by patches of colchicum, or autumn crocus. Much bigger than a spring crocus, the colour splashing across the meadows seemed to leap directly from an Impressionist's canvas. The farmer must take the latest possible hay-cut each year to tide his beasts over the winter. He probably has no interest in the crocuses that bloom as a by-product of this unusual hay-making programme; yet with one pass of his cutter he pleases both his cows and his passers-by! Just for a moment, I almost thought kindly of the Common Agricultural Programme. But only for a moment.

I could happily have wandered all the day along the flower meadows of the Isère Valley. The GR5 would not let me. It led me relentlessly south along the valley of the tributary River Pontardin. A magnificent forest of indigenous trees now guarded the route – huge, centuries-old specimens of ash, oak and walnut, which were under-grown with hazel and aspen. These were the first walnuts I had come across. They have grown here least since Roman times and probably before that, although they did not reach England until the sixteenth century and are still struggling to establish themselves as far north as the Tees.

Sparkling like small jewels at intervals on the ground beneath these big trees is one of my favourite wild-flowers, the Herb Robert. This tiny gem of a wild geranium displays pretty pink flowers from April right through to September. Its parsley-like leaves change from a verdant, emerald green in spring to a polished bronze by autumn. I am so fond of this little darling that I grow it from seed in my greenhouse, pot it on and plant clumps of it all over my garden. Most gardeners dig it up as a weed. Even in gardening I am the odd man out.

There is a string of small villages to tempt the walker onto the east side of the river, yet, inexplicably, the route follows the west bank. This was my day for succumbing to temptation so I decided to walk the east bank and to honour Peysey-Nancroix with my presence for lunch. The restaurant has a terrace with a parlous superstructure of bamboo mats for shade. Perched well above the river and at a height of three thousand feet there are mountain views in all directions. Surrounded by green forests and high mountains, blue skies above and bamboo mats for shade, I could have been in Borneo. Mount Pourri was now ominously close and looking very high. Checking the elevation on the map I came to the discomforting conclusion that between this lunch and the next lay a climb of some five thousand feet. A light lunch seemed sensible in the circumstances so I chose the *Carpaccio de Boeuf* and a light salad, washed down with a lager or two.

After the tribulations of the previous night, it seemed sensible to ring ahead and reserve my accommodation. I had two choices on the route ahead; the easy and the ridiculously easy. This was my rest day so I tried the ridiculously easy option first. They offered me a bed but no food. One meal of unflavoured spaghetti was enough, so I rang the second option. Two hours ahead there was the luxury of a hot shower, a dry bed and a cooked meal. I wanted nothing more.

The Evian-les-Bains camera had indeed proved to be 'most suitable'. Tucked away in a pouch on my belt, I could access it easily and had used up countless rolls of film. Now I needed more film and with the extensive National Park ahead this would be my last opportunity to buy for the next couple of days. The locals assured me that I would get films at the local Tabac which distinguished itself by taking its lunch 'hour' from 12 noon until 3 p.m. Waiting on the steps in the sunshine was no great hardship and in a contented daze I even considered going back for a second *carpaccio*.

Re-stocked with film, I walked out of the village and was surprised to see a railway station. Well, it looked like a railway station, but I knew that the railway line was several miles behind me running through the valley floor beside the River Isère. It turned out to be the village post office. About a hundred years ago the French authorities must have decided to save money on design fees for public buildings. One design fits all. It's an attractive enough design of sensible proportions and simple materials. A blue slate roof with a generous timber eaves caps a straightforward rendered elevation. Happily there are colourful accessories to cheer up the rather dull body; window mullions, curved window arches, and quoined corners all in a shining red brick. Here a post office, there a railway station, elsewhere I daresay a Library or a Mairie. It is a defining part of the French rural scene and I find it attractive.

Beyond the tiny hamlets of Le Moulin and Nancroix lies the vast wilderness of La Vanoise, one of the first and biggest National Parks of France. Just as I thought that the modern world was behind me, I came upon the most extraordinary line of trees. There, leading from roughly nowhere to precisely nowhere is a majestic avenue of trees about half a mile long. The pine trees, now at least 80 feet high, were planted in 1810 to lend status to the house of the Directeur de Mines, which today lies forlorn and semi-derelict at the end of the avenue. The area was once a bustling centre of activity for lead and silver mining. The mines must still have had some value in 1891, when there was an unseemly dispute over who owned what. The claimants laid siege to the incumbents and tried to lay waste to the avenue by sawing at the trunk of every tree. The scars from this act of arboreal vandalism are still visible today but, fortunately, the trees proved to be made of more enduring stuff than the vandals.

The small settlements of the Pontardin valley saw hard times in the twentieth century and the people abandoned the more remote hamlets long ago. Recently, the general prosperity has flowed up the Isère and percolated to these villages. People are moving back to restore abandoned cottages, and the final village of Beaupraz seemed to me to consist entirely of restored homes. Much care has gone into the rebuilding of the stone walls, thick and strong with small windows, they are fine examples of the local architectural tradition. But it all goes wrong with the roofs. Shiny metal roofs turn the old, pastoral settlement of Beaupraz into something more akin to an industrial estate. With such raucous vulgarity screaming at me I hurried away from this misguided economy, saddened by the missed opportunities.

My home for the night, the Refuge de Rosuel, sits like a lodge at the entrance to the Vanoise Parc National. No tin roofs here. The Parc Authority makes a strong statement with this first edifice. The Refuge appears to grow out of the landscape with the side walls built to look like rock faces and a grass roof which continues the line of the hillside above. Inside, it is warm and comfortable, practical and strongly-built. This eco-friendly, harmonious architecture was a timely antidote to Beaupraz and I warmed to the Parc Authority.

The Vanoise is part of a large, international and pioneering conservation project. The Hunter King, Victor Emmanuel II of Italy, started it almost as an act of death-bed remorse. He had hunted to extravagant excess nearly all his life. At the last minute he had a revelation that he alone might be responsible for hunting the alpine ibex into extinction. In the nick of time the killer-turned-conservationist transformed his Royal Hunting Ground into a Protected Area. So it was that in 1922 the Italians led the world with their conservationist agenda by creating the Alpine Reserve of Grand Paradis. Forty years later, the French did their bit by assigning the adjacent region of the Vanoise as a National Park. Whenever, if ever, I see the elusive ibex I must remember to salute King Victor.

Over a beer on the terrace, I joined another international gathering, almost an eisteddfod, with a trio of Welshmen, a pair of Germans and a French biologist. It was a spectacular location for a drink and a chat, dominated by views of the western flank of Mount Pourri. On this side, a massive cliff-face defends the mountain. Above the cliffs, two glaciers cover the upper heights of the mountain and in summer the ice-melt cascades over the cliffs in three dramatic waterfalls, each possibly more than a thousand feet high.

Hans and Freda, dressed in matching black shorts and red tee-shirts, sat cocooned by their shared passion, impervious to the plummeting temperature and oblivious of the Welsh choir crooning in the lounge. Avid birdwatchers, they were glued to binoculars trained on that remote cliff-top, sitting out long after most of the patrons had moved inside for warmth. Their passion was bearded vultures, or lammergeyers According to them, there are only thirty pairs in the whole of the French Alps and they had seen a pair from that very spot. Some of their excitement rubbed off on me and I sat with them in the cold hoping for a rare sighting. Of course, I am not a twitcher, but it is a big bird, the lammergeyer, with the biggest wingspan of any bird in the European skies. It outranks a stork, is almost half as big again as a golden eagle and has a wingspan more than three times that of a kestrel. It is as nasty as it is big. It likes to start its meal with a delicacy, usually the eyes, but sometimes the testicles. It is a bird I prefer to enjoy from a distance, preferably a thousand feet and increasing. For Hans and Freda, seeing lammergeyers well outclassed their earlier sighting of two golden eagles soaring over the same ridge. I vividly recalled watching enormous lammergeyers soaring way above the Pyrenees in recent summers, but equally clearly remembered watching golden eagles floating effortlessly on the thermals in the Scottish Highlands, and I wanted to argue that golden eagles surely were the kings of all things feathered. They have better table manners for a start; they, at least, do not pick your eyes out until you are dead. My limited German and their bright-eyed fanaticism for lammergeyers persuaded me to concede the argument before it started. Instead, I asked them to explain how you can possibly tell an eagle from a vulture when the birds are soaring 2,000 feet above. Apparently it is all in the tail. The eagle has a blunt, three-sided, trapezoidal tail; the vulture, on the other hand, has a pointed, four-sided, rhomboidal tail. Seldom has my knowledge of ornithology, geometry and the German language advanced simultaneously.

Pierre-Jean was a botanist from Normandy and, unlike the rest of us, he was here to work. Tall, gangling and uncoordinated, with stick-out hair and stuck-on clothes, he reminded me of a puppet that had escaped its master. He was studying the ecology of the wetlands in the Vanois Parc. I had not associate wetlands with the high mountains, but there are, of course, lakes, bogs and marshes throughout the hanging valleys.

Chapter Ten

I Hate Ski Resorts

La Vanoise Parc welcomed me with acres of colour. Large clumps of deep purple cranesbill cheered me on my way, their vibrant colour a contrast to the shy, pastel blue cranesbill that I encourage in my garden. I worried that the climb to the Col du Palet would be long and hard, yet it turned out to be anything but. I set off through groves of wind-stunted alder, interlaced with rowans dripping with bunches of brilliant, scarlet-red berries. Rowans are such good value in the mountains. In the winter their silver-grey trunks gleam against the snow, in spring they bring an early show of light green to a grey world of rock and moor, by late summer they are alight with berries, yet it is in autumn that they reach their glory. By then, they are fire-bursts of red and golden leaves dotted across the hillside, like beacons calling the fyrd to battle. Under the alders grew thickets of wild redcurrant and raspberry. The berries of both looked ripe and tempting, but were disappointingly pithy and too sour to be worth the effort of picking.

This woodland gave way gradually to a denser larch forest with little undergrowth and no variety. I struggled up a steep path, climbing a rocky promontory to gain a long, relatively flat section as the path passed through a hanging-valley. A manoeuvre I had to repeat several times to reach the top. In the first hanging valley, there was Pierre-Jean in his beloved wetland, kneeling in the mud excitedly trying to identify a stalk of grass that was new to him and, he thought, new to the Vanois Parc. It looked pretty ordinary to me, but to Pierre-Jean it represented a major discovery and a personal triumph.

The alpine level starts at about seven thousand feet, where the average temperature is a cheery zero degrees. A few undernourished grasses and tiny, star-shaped saxifrages make brave efforts, but there are no rowans or cranesbill to add colour here.

The great slopes of rock scree sweeping down from Mont Pourri were close at hand and I could hear the clatter of stones way above me. There must be chamois and ibex moving about up there, though I could not see them. This was decidedly unfair because I was sure they could see me. I was so eager to see ibex in the wild that I thought of making a climb to try and get above the scree, but common sense prevailed.

A rare display of flowers took my mind off the invisible ibex. A small patch of edelweiss was thriving just beside the path. Needing an excuse for a breather, I sat down, the better to examine it. I had walked for days across carpets of the most colourful and striking flowers. The gentians, campanula, orchids, clematis and aquilegia of the French Alps are the basis of so much of the English herbaceous border and yet the pale and uninteresting edelweiss is chosen as the alpine floral emblem. I studied it carefully, but still could not see was all the fuss about. It looked to me very much like a dishevelled ox-eye daisy. Looking around me, the truth dawned and I gave the little plant the great credit it deserves. None of the colourful grandiose plants grow anywhere near this tough alpine altitude, but the edelweiss does. It triumphs in a climate that has ruthlessly eliminated all but the botanically small and robust. I could see a few saxifrages with minute flowers hugging the ground, but they were so small that the bees must need binoculars to find them. In contrast, the edelweiss appears to produce elephantine blooms of large, white-petalled flowers with what look like yellow centres. Pierre-Jean, or any botanist, would tell you that the tiny yellow centres are, in reality, clusters of very small flowers and the white edges are simply swollen bracts pretending to be petals. By this clever illusion edelweiss produce a bee-attractor some hundred times larger and more successful than the saxifrage.

The climb finished at Col du Palet after a series of rocky faces separated by small stony pastures. By gaining the col, I had at last overcome Mount Pourri, which had dominated my route since that celebratory lunch two days ago. The next mountain to the south, the great mass of La Grande Motte would be my task-master for the next couple of days. Nestled into the rock face just below the col was a Refuge. Built in timber in the Swiss chalet style, it looked welcoming and I began to salivate at thoughts of an early, leisurely lunch. Alas, the cook was away getting groceries on her three-wheeled motorcycle. She would not be back for some time; certainly there would be no lunch for at least two hours. I never had much patience and the gourmet restaurant of Val Claret, just an hour away in the valley below, beckoned.

Decision time. The GR5 route continues westwards through the ski resort of Val d'Isère before turning south again through the Reserve de L'Iseran. Another route, the GR55, goes more directly south avoiding most of the resorts. Both routes meet again near Modane in L'Arc Valley. The main GR5 has the advantage of offering two or three days of peaceful trekking in the remote mountains against the disadvantage of an afternoon trudging through ski-resorts. On the other hand, the less-interesting GR55 would get me to Modane a day or so earlier, avoiding the ski resorts. I was not short of time and I would probably see ibex in the Reserve de L'Iseran. Perhaps I should take the long route.

As I was mulling over these issues I covered two hundred years in twenty minutes. I left a nineteenth century world of quiet pasture, goats and mountains to enter the twenty-first century world of hubbub, helicopters, cars and cranes. The delicate sounds of bird-song and waterfalls were replaced by a coarse cacophony of ghetto-blasters and revving engines.

How I hate ski resorts. Their developers litter beautiful mountain valleys with endless rows of ugly metallic skeletons chained to one another with loops of cable. They build cube after boring cube of flats in utter disregard for the local architectural tradition. They develop main streets with garish lights promoting hideous Pizzerias, Bars, Restaurants and Ski-Clothing Shops. These are the very operators who flaunt in their brochures the beauty of a landscape they have destroyed with their developments. Having made their mess, they clear off for the summer, leaving a ghost town. As I walked down the hill back into the Isère Valley, I tried not to be a Grumpy Old Man and see it from the other side. I would no doubt have sold out to the devil if I were a poor shepherd with nothing but a few goats which made little contribution to feeding my family. I tried to visualise the place in the winter – it must be great fun with the snow, the lights and crowds of people enjoying themselves.

In this rare mood of reasonableness, I walked into town at high noon on a hot summer's day, longing for a drink. I trekked around a Marie Celeste of a town – not a restaurant, not a bar was open. The only evidence of human presence was the noise of building. What a nightmare! What a dump! What a contrast to the Abondance Valley. I do not know what Val Claret looks like in winter. I hope that the snow and the fairy-lights create a magical atmosphere for the people who pay good money to stay there. In the summer it is the pits: a depression in the mountains sprouting ugly, rectangular blocks of buildings. There is not a blade of grass, not a stunted tree, not a reason for joy in sight. An abandoned coal-mine in 1960s County Durham was a beauty spot in comparison. There was not even a water tap. Eminent reasonableness, my foot! I hate ski resorts.

At least my decision about the route was easy to make. Not for me an afternoon of trudging through more deserted resorts. I would take the short route south, straight into the hills and scurry back into the haven of the wilderness.

I trudged out of town and sat on a rock for my lunch. This was not the gourmet meal I had anticipated, but I could still treat myself to a fine, *al fresco* meal of the delicacy I had bought at Bellentre, the sardines soaked in chilli peppers. With some two-day old bread and plenty of fresh water I would have a feast. Except that, since there had been no taps in the town, I had only two cups of water left and rationed myself to one to wash down the whole meal. Sardines in chilli take a great deal of washing down and, with my throat on fire, I reluctantly had to leave half of them.

With peppery throat, I started to climb out of L'Isère Valley on that hot afternoon and it soon became obvious that there was no running water available. The northern side of La Grande Motte, the great, glaciated fortress of a mountain between me and the rest of the world, was dry. There was not a trickle in the stream beds. I faced four hours walking, three of them uphill, with a burning throat and only a cupful of water. A strict water management strategy was called for. I usually find that the more I drink in high temperatures, the more I want to drink, so I resolved to climb for three hours to the top without stopping, saving my whole cupful of water for the ridge, then descend helter-skelter to the Refuge.

The flora on this section was so beautiful that it was easy to forget my thirst. Here, the gentian reigned supreme. Luxuriant, deep blue, trumpet-shaped flowers sprang from arid rocks. They highlighted the route in infrequent patches, each patch so bright that it looked from a distance as if somebody had spilt a tin of fluorescent paint. Struggling in vain to compose the definitive ode to the gentian, I eventually gained the northern shoulder of La Grande Motte, a mountain three-times as high as Ben Nevis and every bit as regal. On the col, drinking my cup of water in restrained sips, I looked back fondly on Tarentais with its shining onion-spires and enormous hay-lofts. Looking ahead, I wondered what I might find to interest and entertain me in the Maurienne.

No water-butt with swan-neck fountain was ever more welcome than the one which sits at the centre of the cluster of huts that make up Refuge de Laisse. Two German couples watched in amusement as I plunged my head deep into the ice-cold water and blew bubbles for as long as my breath lasted. Then I took my pack off. After I had showered and washed my clothes, the older of the couples proudly led me to some edelweiss flowering on a bank beside the Refuge.

'There, Sir. Do you see the white flower?'

'You mean the edelweiss?'

They were crestfallen to find I was already acquainted with the plant. For a second night I was in the company of two obsessed Germans; this time Johanne and Inga from Bremen, whose passion was not bearded vultures but mountain flowers. Abandoning the edelweiss, they launched instead into a detailed lecture on Alpine Clovers. By sneaking a quick look at the sub-titles in their book I knew that they were talking about yellow-bay clover, pink meadow clover and white mountain clover. They all sound delightful, but I cannot recognise any of them unless they are in flower. The two of them were so animated and enthusiastic that I tried to show interest and disguise the fact that I understood virtually nothing of their dissertation.

Seven of us sat down to dinner that night, two Belgians, four Germans and an odd Englishman; all sharing a love of the mountains. We may have struggled to find common language but, knowing instinctively that we had shared values, we appreciated each other's company.

Bang. Our tranquillity was shattered. Two Americans burst in, all noise and bustle. Unwashed and unchanged from a full day's trek in the sun they sat down to dinner with us. Before introductions even had been attempted, one pulled out a video camera, switched on an extremely bright light and without a 'by your leave', blinded us as he panned the assembled company with the commentary, 'These are the folks we had dinner with at Refuge Lacey'.

He switched the machine off and announced to the table at large, 'We've come from Lake Geneva in seven days, what are you guys doing?'

Without waiting for a reply he informed us, 'We're going to Modane tomorrow. I know the book says it is two days, but we'll do it in one; these mountains are pretty easy.'

That was it. No introductions. No courtesies. No apology for smelly bodies. Once we got to the soup, they discussed between themselves, in dominant voices, the logistics of their trip tomorrow. Before they had arrived the seven of us had been struggling to establish conversation with scraps of English, French and German. It was impossible for us to continue above those two strident voices. We supped our soup in silence.

Half way through the meat course, I rebelled at their boorish behaviour. 'Have you seen any gentians on your trek?' I asked.

'Gentians? What the hell are gentians?'

'Probably the most beautiful flower that you will ever see. They are quite common on the heights so you must have seen them frequently on the edge of the path today.'

'No, we ain't got time to look at flowers,' said Yankee One.

One of the Germans took up the attack. 'Have you seen many butterflies in the mountains?'

'Yeah, we seen lots of butterflies, Dunno what they were,' replied Yankee Two.

The young Belgian girl delicately delivered the *coup de grâce*. 'And have you seen chamois?'

The penny dropped. They looked around, open-mouthed, finally realising that we were in the mountains for very different reasons to theirs and that they had not only failed to establish any bond with us, but had created a thinly-disguised hostility. The Swankee Yankees lapsed into silence and we were able to continue our halting but courteous conversation.

Chapter Eleven

The King of the Alps

The Americans woke me indecently early, having a heated discussion about their sat-nav equipment. Arguments about equipment at seven in the morning are definitely not cricket! If I did not like the word 'sat-nav' before, I positively loathed it now. Awake, but unenthusiastic about getting up, I lay and thought about the effect of technological advances on our language. The Continentals are developing new words to keep abreast of the technological revolution with rather more panache than the English. Thank goodness for a little Gallic style. I am not particularly eager to visit a '*graphidermiste*' but he sounds more of a gentleman than a 'tattooist'. I have never paid to be fried on a sunbed, but I rather like the idea of exposing myself to some '*bronzage*'. Our word 'mobile-phone' lacks imagination; the Italians' '*telefonetto*' makes you smile just to hear it. What woman in her right mind with the opportunity for a little, discreet 'epilation' would bother with the services of a vulgar 'eyebrow-plucker'. Finally the Swankee-Yankees packed up their gear with their bad manners and departed; now I could get back to peace with the world.

The clover-lovers had left the Refuge before me but I found them a little way along the path intently scanning the ground.

'Have you lost something?'

'Oh no,' said Inga, matter-of-factly. 'We collect stones.'

Why, I wondered? Were we in an area of geological rarities? Were there dinosaurs' eggs for the finding?

'Are you looking for fossils?'

'Oh no. We collect stones for our *enkel*, for our grandchildren,' she said, looking up at me with a smile. She showed me a small black pebble with a vein of quartz. It was pretty, but I did not see anything remarkable about it. She told me that every day she collected a stone for each of her grandchildren. She had three grandchildren and was out walking for ten days. A quick weight calculation of thirty grammes per pebble, for my five grandchildren on this fourteen day walk, convinced me that I could never match her grand-parental devotion.

Initially, my route took me in the shadow of the enormous masses of La Grande Motte and its partner La Grande Casse which together form a massive sweep of mountain to the north, defining the Laisse valley as it joins the Valley de Termignon. It was some way up on the cliffs of this great rampart that I saw him; a magnificent stag ibex. Presumably some slight movement against the light had caught my eye because I had heard nothing. He was a long way away, but he was unmistakeable, standing still and proud in silhouette. His horns, dark and curved like a scimitar, looked enormous even from this distance. I learned afterwards that they were probably a metre long. It was not a close encounter, but I did not care; I trembled with excitement and under my breath sang the praises of King Victor. Usually the males travel in small bachelor parties during the summer and I waited, hoping that more would appear. When it was apparent the stag was on his own, I rushed back to Inga and Johanne with the news and they came running. We gazed breathlessly for several minutes until the beast gracefully withdrew from sight.

'Finding an ibex is better than finding a clover –yes?' I teased my German friends.

'Ya, an ibex is better than an edelwiess. For sure.'

It was for me the highlight of two weeks of walking. I danced on the spot with elation. I had seen the King of the Alps, however distantly.

By mid-morning, I reached the Refuge at Plan du Lac, which claimed my affection on two counts. Firstly, a most charming mademoiselle was in charge. Secondly, it looked the ultimate in chocolate-box pictures. Huge, roughly-trimmed tree trunks supported the low pitched roof. Timber-balustraded balconies dripped with brightly coloured flowers in large plant-boxes. The whole effect was of strength, colour and cheerfulness; it was a defiant architectural statement declaring 'we might be small humans in a daunting wilderness, but we are not overwhelmed'. Mademoiselle served a jumbo-sized *café au lait* and made me a couple of sandwiches for lunch.

There is an unusual and rare cow on these high pastures, and, of course, in France, another kind of cow means another kind of cheese. The Tarine is a beast distinguished by a fawn coat with unusual brown rings, usually around the eyes. The cheese is a soft, blue-veined delight, the Termignon. I am an enthusiast for soft blues and am not surprised that its ancient recipe a closely-guarded secret.

I crossed the tree-line as the path came down the mountainside into the Valley de L'Arc and very quickly the tree-growth became luxuriant. There were so many paths and forest tracks zigzagging ahead that I knew I was likely to get lost. So what? As long as I was going downhill and roughly southwards. In fact, I was glad I *did* get lost because, in my meanderings, I came across a spectacular waterfall. I sat beneath it, dabbling my hot feet in a cold pool, and unpacked the sandwiches of Madamoiselle du Plan du Lac. 'Sandwich'? Each so-called sandwich was composed of three slices of bread, at least eight inches across; one filled with two thick layers of moist, fresh pâté, the other with two generous slices of creamy Termignon. With a continuous cascade of sparkling water at my disposal, for drinking and washing, I had an infinitely better lunch than the day before. What a refreshing and generous introduction to the gastronomic delights of the Maurienne.

The valley woodland became ever more luxuriant as I neared the bottom of the hill. As the contours began to level out I knew that civilisation must be close. The first sign of it to greet me was not the usual abandoned rusty tractor nor the ubiquitous piles of builder's rubble but something knew to me. Valezan had greeted me with a flying escort of butterflies and grasshoppers. Termignon welcomed me with a Sentier Médicin; a Herbal Footpath, complete with a course in Alternative Medicine! Every twenty yards or so, for a couple of kilometres around a circular path, was a discreet notice-board with an illustrated description of a wild plant, presumably growing close at hand, and information on the multitude of ailments and afflictions that the particular plant would cure. What a marvellous idea!

I walked eagerly into Termignon looking forward to a beer on a flowered terrace overlooking the river. It was not to be. In early September, Termignon was grey, miserable and unwelcoming, without a flower in sight. I might have found a use for my colour film at the jewel of the town, the Chapel of the Visitation. Even that was miserable today; it was undergoing restoration, hidden under scaffolding and flapping, plastic sheeting. There was some consolation. The eastern end was at an advanced stage of completion and a Baroque dome, most exquisitely-proportioned, poked out of the sheeting, gleaming with its new paint in the afternoon sun. A pink-rendered, octagonal tower burst through an unexceptional, tiled roof. The perfect proportions of the tower were emphasised by its cupola; a curving delight of small slates as exquisitely shaped as an inverted, eight-petalled bellflower.

Termignon was closed but I did manage to procure a beer from an grim-faced Patron – how on earth do these people get into the hospitality business? The next village could hardly be less welcoming. Case-hardened by a France that had turned its back on the summer with unsmiling patrons, dead ski resorts and closed auberges; I rang a Gîte d'Etape, two hours walk away. '*Pas de problem,*' was the answer to all my questions about beds, showers and meals. And so it turned out.

Down the valley, in the tiny settlement of Sollières, I spotted a couple whose Englishness leaped out at me from a hundred yards. She had that infuriating habit of walking along looking at the ground with her arms folded across her chest. How is it that tall, elegant and graceful women throw away their God-given poise and walk with downcast look and rounded shoulders. Bring back finishing schools, deportment lessons and balancing books on heads.

Patrick and Judy from Somerset were holidaying in their parents' cottage nearby. They were full of the gossip and jokes of the British ex-pat community. Generally this bores me to death, but I could not resist the contagious humour of these two. My favourite story concerned the rumours that abounded in Britain and France just before the enlargement of the European Union. Particularly virulent in France was the rumour about Polish plumbers, which probably spread at a speed in inverse proportion to its truthfulness. According to rumour, there were hordes of Polish plumbers massed on the borders, ready to invade France to work at Polish rates of pay and in the process put out of work the noble, quality-conscious, highly-trained and dedicated-to-the-customer French plumbers. Fearful for their way of life, the French plumbers were up in arms across the nation; waving their pipe-wrenches and swinging their ball-cocks! The Polish Embassy read the situation and disarmed it with aplomb. They put up posters across France showing a most attractive, well-muscled, bare-chested young Polish plumber with the caption 'I am too busy – you come and see me!' In the event, come enlargement of the EU, there was no noticeable invasion. But there has been a significant increase in the number of young, female, French tourists visiting Poland.

Monsieur Pas-de-Problem ran Les Glaciers in Bramans. This is an unusual establishment – that rare combination of a Gîte d'Etape and a Logis Restaurant under the same roof and the same management. Both Gîtes d'Etape and Logis are French establishments which provide many of the things that I enjoy about the French way of life, yet neither type of establishment has managed to take root on the English side of the Channel. At first thoughts that is a great pity. On second thoughts, I am more than happy for France to stay very French and so be different to England.

Monsieur smiled at every opportunity. Obviously powered by those longer-life batteries, he literally left the average hotel-manager standing; continuously on the move, he attended to every detail of the running of his establishment. On top of that he had youthful, Gallic good looks with curly, fair hair and a dapper moustache. No wonder his hotel was so popular; I was not surprised that he was still doing a roaring trade when most of France had closed for the winter.

I shared the facilities with a party of twenty young German cyclists – the serious-minded sort with ultra-lightweight bicycles, streamlined safety-hats, shiny pants and earnest, heated discussions over route-maps. I can boast to have done a bit of cycling in my time. In my baggy, khaki shorts astride my sit-up-and-beg bicycle with its sophisticated three-speed gear-change, I have fearlessly crossed whole counties, if not continents. In spite of this manifest evidence of an experienced and sophisticated cycling past, I had slight misgivings whether young Hans might welcome me into his club. Which, upon consideration, is only recognition of reality since he and his friends would be a good twenty miles ahead of me after the first hour.

Monsieur Pas de Problem fulfilled his promises, and more, with regard to the dinner. He provided a banquet fit for a king. The meal started with a *Fondant de St Jacques et Croustillantes de Langoustines* which was clearly suitable for a pilgrim like me. Delicate in flavour and contrasting in texture, something was definitely lost in the translation to its English description as 'Scallop blanc-mange with Chinese crackers'. Is it any wonder that English restaurants describe food in French? The main course of *Magret de Canard au miel et gingembre,* served with courgettes, tomatoes and celeriac was heavenly. The cheeseboard was a reunion with old friends, a diary map of the delights of the GR5. It started with mild and creamy Abondance from the first valley, moved on to a fine Beaufort Gruyere Vallee d'Isère and finished with soft blue-yellow Termignon from just up the road. From the sweet trolley I selected prune tart with custard and meringues; the plate was just too small for the ice-cream! I had chosen a bottle of Apremont R Masson. That particular terrace has produced wine since 1471, but my bottle was none the worse for being a 2004 vintage.

It seemed ungracious to leave anything in the bottle so I sat savouring it and mulling over my day. I realised that I was only a couple of hours walk from Modane and that I could easily have got there; quite possibly before those Swankee-Yankees. But what was the rush? In any case, the town was not big enough for the three of us.

Chapter Twelve

Hannibal, Napoleon and Me

There was trouble ahead. As I left Bramans I could hear a clamour of shrieks coming from the woods. Either a brass band was tuning up, or somebody was being cruelly murdered, or both. It turned out to be a brassy band of birds; jays, crows, magpies and woodpeckers were all competing noisily to prove that they had the harshest of calls. Once my ears had adjusted to the sounds I realised there was no competition; nothing sounds as raucous and is as unattractive as a jay. The cause of the pandemonium was likely to be a prowling predator; perhaps a fox or even an elusive pine marten. The birds were probably mobbing it and forcing it to move on. I inched forward quietly in the hope of spotting the creature, but I had no luck.

I had some decisions to make today. This was a walk of two halves, two weeks in successive summers. The first half was coming to an end and I needed to decide today where to finish this first stage of my walking. I was engrossed with my options rather than with the scenery. I had to fly home from Geneva in three days time. Option one was to take a convenient rail connection from Modane to

Geneva which would allow me a couple of days of leisure on the route. Option two was to continue to the next rail link on the GR5 at Briançon from where there is a rather tenuous rail link back to Geneva. Briançon was two, maybe three, days walk ahead, so that it was hard walk, with a long train journey and no days off.

I wanted to be home. Grown men shouldn't get homesick yet strong emotions were stirring. The lawns needed cutting, the hedges wanted trimming and surely Jo would need my advice on the garden by now? Absorbed in my thoughts I walked as if blindfolded through the lovely wooded valley of L'Arc. A shadow brought me back to reality.

An animal flitted across the path in front; it was dark, possibly black, about squirrel-size with a long and fluffy tail. As I neared the point on the track where it had crossed, there was a jay screeching continually to my right. The black shadow skittered up a tree, paused, skittered again then crouched, watching. Surely these were the movements of a predator – a predatee would have kept right on skittering away to safety.

The jay kept screeching, more worried about the black shape than about me. The creature turned towards me and I could see little white stick-up ears and a yellowy-white bib. It was a pine marten. Why this nocturnal creature was cavorting about in broad daylight was a puzzle; possibly it was hungry and on the hunt for a young chick for breakfast. Two new species of mammals in two days – another of the pleasures of walking in the Alps.

Just before Modane on the west side of the L'Arc Valley is the Fort de l'Esseillon built in tiers as it steps up the hillside above a gorge. This is no medieval ruin, and bears similarities to the late eighteenth century defence works built at Berwick-on-Tweed at the time of the threat of Napoleonic invasion. You can understand the hows and whys of defending a seaport. The logic behind a terracing of forts facing across a river to a mountain was not so easy to understand. Who was defending themselves against whom in this valley at that time? My meagre knowledge of European history provided no answers. I was discombobulated. My motto, 'never walk past an unanswered question' decided me; there was nothing for it, Briançon would have to wait until next year; I would go across the valley and investigate.

From a protected entry-gate beside the River L'Arc, the fortifications are built in tiers up the hillside. Today, close to, the buildings have all the appeal of a Victorian prison. It took me a long time to work out why these buildings were here, but gradually I pieced together the story.

Despite the fact that these buildings had their backs to the wall and faced east, they were not designed to defend France against an enemy coming over the mountains directly in front, since there never was an enemy that stupid. No, the buildings were built to control movement of troops in the L'Arc Valley, which at this point runs north-south but which, a few miles to the north, turns east to cross the Alps at the Mont Cenis Pass at 7,000 feet. This is a highly strategic pass into Italy, quite possibly used by Hannibal and his elephants on his circuitous attack on Rome.

So, the Hapsburgs built the first of the present fortifications to defend the far south-western corner of the Austro-Hungarian Empire against France. I was in France today, but I was standing on yesterday's line between Hapsburgs and Bourbons. A line which, in its time, was as decisive and perhaps almost as divisive as the Iron Curtain has been to my generation.

By the time of the French Republic, France was taking all before it and the young Napoleon came this way. Recognising the strategic importance of the Mont Cenis Pass, he worked on improving the roads in the L'Arc Valley, the better to attack Italy. With the fall of the French Republic, Savoie became Italian, part of the Kingdom of Piedmont, centred on Milan. It was King Victor Emmanuel I of Piedmont who built these extensive fortifications between 1817 and 1834. Strangely, Italians built these elaborate defences to contain Frenchmen, rather than the other way round. All of which seems to have been yet another

From the starting point at Lake Geneva, the first day took me past footpath shrines at St Gingolph (*above right*), then out of the town and into the valley beyond (*below*).

Day 2: The happy family of Neuteu came out to cheer me on my way.

Day 3: The hills are alive with the sound of cowbells on Mont de Grange (*below*).

Day 4: The church at Samoens, the town of seven mountains (*bottom*).

Day 6: The Dome du Gouter, seen from the Hotel at La Prarion, pure and sparkling in the sunlight.

Day 9: The spectacular view from the terrace of the Refuge de Roseul, a fine place for a reviving beer.

Day 10: Do not dawdle on the flank of Mont Pourri – you might ossify.

Day 11: A fine example of French civic pride is seen here in Valley de l'Arc.

Day 15: Eventually, on weary legs, I reached the Refuge at Mont Thabor.

Day 15: The turquoise water of the lake above les Granges sparkles
invitingly (*above*); "If you knew this was your last hour, you would not
go fishing", the *cardan solaire* at Plampinet (*below left*); Pointe Gaspard
towers protectively over Les Granges (*below right*).

Day 17: The historic
centre of Briançon is
strongly fortified. This
picturesque town is an *al
fresco* art gallery of *cadran
solaires.*

Day 20: From the forest above Ceillac there was no obvious way out to the south.

Day 23: The town of St Etienne de Tinée has narrow streets of four storey, terraced buildings in attractive renders.

Day 24: I was on top of the world again, walking through a wildflower meadow above Auron.

Day 25: The path drops from the larch parkland, alongside the waterfall above Roure.

example of a defence budget being a colossal waste of taxpayers' money, since the Italians and the French were allies for the rest of the nineteenth century. Indeed, during the Crimean War, Italy, France and Britain were fighting on the same side for the first time in history. When Victor Emmanuel II became the King of a united Italy in 1860 he owed a debt to two key supporters. The first was his good friend Garibaldi, who united the Italian states and handed him the crown on a plate (or perhaps, on a cushion). The second was his latter-day ally, the French who had fought beside the Italians to drive the Austrians back across the Alps, so that he could safely wear his crown. In appreciation, Victor Emmanuel II ceded the Duchy of Savoie to France, including all the extravagant castles and defences his father had built in the Valley d'Arc.

Sitting at one end of the tunnels linking France and Italy through the mountains, Modane appeared to be a town to hurry through rather than to linger in. It lacks the old town centre with dignified public buildings that normally distinguish small French towns. With this lack of architectural interest or the civic cheerfulness which I had grown used to in towns like Samoens, there was no inducement to stay. I would finish this year's trek here and take the train back to Geneva, sampling the delights of Champery and Aix-les-Bains on the way. Decision made, I sat at a café-table still reluctant to tear myself away from my GR5. I scanned the mountains to the south visually working out the route for the start of next year's trip. The path must go under that railway line and then under the high viaduct that carries the motorway into Italy, before it wanders ever southwards into the peace and quiet on the flanks of Mont Thabor.

That railway line was the site of the World's Worst Rail Disaster Ever. A thousand French soldiers were returning from fighting in North Italy for Christmas in 1917. There was a shortage of rolling stock. The troops crammed themselves into nineteen carriages which needed four locomotives to pull them. Only one was available. The imperious military command over-ruled the experienced railway management. One engine may be slow but it will get them home, said the military. The railwaymen knew that one engine could not control nineteen loaded coaches, particularly when sixteen of them had no brakes.

'Drive or be shot,' was the choice given to the train driver.

He drove. The train climbed slowly through the Alps to Modane where it followed the line down into the valley bottom at gradients of 1 in 33, steep for a steam train. The braking power of one engine was no match for the momentum of the nineteen, heavily loaded carriages. The train, out of control, went faster and faster until, at 75 miles per hour, the first coach derailed. The other eighteen wooden coaches rammed into it, catching fire. Of the eight hundred men killed, five hundred were burned beyond recognition.

I had a cup of strong black coffee as I visualised the carnage on that hillside, with horse-drawn ambulances slowly taking the wounded to hospitals miles away. I was thankful that I was flying home.

Had that rail accident got to me or was I just sad to be at the end of my trip for this year? Either way it was time to snap out of it. I re-ran the highlights of my walk; ibex and chamois, woodpeckers and vultures, gentians and edelweiss. By the time I remembered the Cheshire Chavs and Mr Effing Upping, I was almost laughing out loud. With a grin on my face, I forced myself away from the wonders and joys of the GR5 and wandered into the bustle of Modane railway station. After twelve days of peace in the mountains it was time to go home and sort out the gardener.

Chapter Thirteen

From Bad to Bardonecchio

Half-asleep, I tossed and turned in my bed. Twelve months had passed since I walked into that railway station in Modane and I was going back to the French Alps in the morning. Packing lists were scrolling through my mind. Had I packed the washing-powder and the clothes-pegs? Did I have both those sets of pills in silver-foil, the ones to open and the others to close crucial valves in critical situations? Would I have enough socks? If I know that I have to get up at a reasonable hour, I sleep soundly until the cursed alarm awakes me. If I know that I have to get up at an ungodly hour like 4.30 a.m., then I wake at midnight, and every hour thereafter, thrashing around until the sweet alarm brings welcome relief from the torment.

So it was on the morning of my return to the GR5. Short of sleep, bleary-eyed and grumpy I may have been, but I was on the aeroplane and ready to go by 7 a.m. Congestion in the air over the London area kept us grounded for an hour.

My journey had hardly begun and already I had a problem. Even if all had gone to plan, it would have been tight getting to

Nice station in time to board the one and only train that would deliver me to Modane this day. If I missed the train I would lose a day of walking. I sat in the lounge at Newcastle Airport and went through my packing lists again.

Once airborne, a tail-wind enabled us to make up time. I ran out of the terminal just in time to see the back of the bus to Nice pulling away. Determined to regain my schedule, I took a taxi. For a not inconsiderable sum the driver deposited me on the doorstep of the Gare de Nice ten minutes before my train was due to leave. Plenty of time. In the central concourse a mass of people, comfortably ensconced in armchairs, were patiently watching large display screens. A pretty mademoiselle gave me a slip of paper with a number. The display screens showed which number-holder was to report to which of the half a dozen enquiry desks around the sides of the hall. Instead of shuffling along in a queue dragging baggage, people lolled in armchairs. What a superb system.

I had ticket number 279 and the number on the display screen was 196. There were six desks to serve the 83 people ahead of me, and my train left in nine minutes. I went back to the pretty mademoiselle and explained my predicament. She calmly directed me to an entirely different ticket hall on the other side of the concourse, which was solely for the benefit of travellers leaving within the hour. Here the queues were small and the number of ticket-issuers high. I asked for a ticket to Modane, France via Turin, Italy. In no time I had my ticket together with a personalised, printed schedule of my three-stage journey from Nice to Modane. I was on the train with seconds to spare, silently praising the courtesy and efficiency of the SNCF.

I crossed into Italy, arriving at Ventimiglia easily enough, but I could find no reference on the departure board to the Turin train listed on my printed schedule. An Italian official studied my schedule carefully and grinned broadly.

'Ah Monsieur. The French Railway lady has given you a very good programme.' Pause for effect.

'From the Winter Timetable.' Further pause for the *coup de grâce*.

'It was summer yesterday, officially. Ha, ha.'

When he tired of his joke, he took great delight in telling me, 'Never mind, my friend. You are lucky. You are in Italy.'

The train to Turin had just left and the next was in two hours. He would re-schedule my journey to get me to my destination tonight.

'Go and enjoy the town, have some lunch, see the sea.'

He went off, chuckling to himself over French incompetence, leaving me with two hours to kill in Ventimiglia.

Within minutes of leaving the station I was sitting in a restaurant overlooking the Mediterranean, white wine in hand, blue sky above, with nothing to interrupt my view other than the topless beauties oiling themselves on the beach below. The Salad Niçoise came up to expectations. Better dressed than the languid beauties, the salty flavour of tuna combined well with the vinaigrette and its oily allure. Next time I break a journey at Ventimiglia, it will be for two weeks not two hours. I strolled back to the station thinking of Mussolini and accurate timetables.

Alerted by some sixth sense, I tried to buy a map of the Italian National Railway System in the station bookstall but I could only find one like a London Underground map in a pocket diary, too small to be of much use to a stranger. The duty official had changed, but he knew all about me and the wrong French schedule.

'You had the wrong schedule from the bad, French lady – ha ha ha! Here is the right schedule from the good Italian man. Ha ha ha.'

'Quickly, quickly, your train is in the station.' The ever-helpful official hustled me on to the 14.58 to Voghara. I was curious; there was no mention of Turin in my Schedule and I had never heard of Voghara. When I could find no reference to it on my Railway Map I felt distinctly uncomfortable. I asked a fellow passenger to locate

Voghara on my map. He stubbed his finger at a point due east, way beyond Genoa, yet I needed to go practically due north to Turin. I jumped off the train just as it pulled out. Then I learned that my new schedule on the current timetables from the ultra-efficient Italian Railway Officials routed me to Modena in Italy whereas I wanted to go to Modane in France. Ha, ha, ha, my foot!

A third official gave me a revised schedule based on the current summer timetable, to Modane in France via Turin which is what I had asked for in the first place.

At last, I was on the move again, apparently in the right direction. The scenery on the route north from Ventimiglia was outstanding and more than justified the frustration over tickets, timetables and schedules. The terrain was immediately seriously mountainous. The line cuts its way through shoulders of rock along steep, almost sheer-sided ravines, as often as not through tunnels, a remarkable feat of engineering.

I was sitting on the floor. I had given up my seat to one of a group of garrulous old ladies who had just overrun the carriage. They were returning home from a shopping trip in a happy mood and were chattering loudly and simultaneously. In stark contrast, the glum ticket inspector looked morosely at my ticket and silently held out his hand. In my enthusiasm to get on the right train at Ventimiglia, I had omitted to present my ticket to the franking machine at the entry to the platform. This is a serious offence in Italy for which there is an on-the-spot fine of five Euros. Enough is enough. I gave up all attempts to speak in any foreign language and in icily-polite, softly-spoken English I gave him the full catalogue of my misfortunes with transport in general and trains in particular, most especially with Railway Officials and Schedules. I told him quietly that I would not give him five Euros and, holding my wrists up in submission, I invited him to arrest me. Nobody in the crowded carriage understood a word I said, but the old biddies were on my side. Had I not given dear Paola my seat? Walking sticks at the ready, they hectored the Inspector in Italian that was possibly less than icily-polite. The inspector shrugged and gave up the unequal struggle. He angrily clicked my ticket and stomped on his way without the five Euros.

At last I arrived in Turin some fifteen hours after that alarm call. The revised-revised schedule allowed me ten minutes to decide whether I wanted to stop overnight in Turin or continue to the border town of Bardonecchia. The station was bleak and distinctly unwelcoming and I could find no information about hotels. It would be far easier to find reasonable accommodation late in the evening in a small town than in a big city. Bardonecchia it would be.

As a general rule, generalisations get me into trouble. Generally, it would have been easy to find accommodation in Bardonecchia but, at the time of my arrival, Italy was playing Ghana in the Football World Cup. As a result, I arrived in a ghost-town with the sun setting on flapping signs in empty streets. But I found a hotel. The receptionist booked me in, his left eye on me, his right glued to the TV screen. The cook had both eyes on the football, so the squinting receptionist palmed me off to a pizzeria around the corner. Fortunately for me, the young waitress there had no interest in football and she served me with great attentiveness, as if to make a point to the noisy group of lads crouched around the TV set in the adjacent bar.

With a small carafe of Chianti to finish, I mulled over my frustrating day. I was once travelling in Japan, well away from the tourist routes. I presented the young girl who was dispensing the tickets in the bus station with a piece of paper on which was written, in Roman script, the name of the town I wanted to reach. Mutely, she took out her own piece of paper and started to draw. First she drew a bus stop with the letter 'C' on it, so that I knew at which of the six bus stops I had to wait. Then she drew a bus with a number on it, so that I knew which bus to catch. Beside the bus she wrote a time in the 24-hour clock and beneath that another time. Clearly they were the times of departure and arrival of my bus. Finally she wrote down another number put a 'Y' beside it, encircled it with a flourish and, smiling, held out her hand for the fare. She had given me all the information that I needed without fuss or confusion. I hope that by now she is Chief Executive Officer of the Yokohama Perpetual Sunshine Bus Company.

If today was a taste of things to come, perhaps I should turn round and go home. It had all the ingredients of a holiday from hell. But tomorrow I would enjoy, all the more, the tranquillity and peace of the mountains. Or so I told myself!

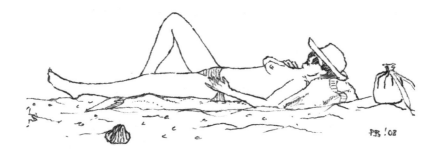

Chapter Fourteen

Skinny Dipping

The Frejus Tunnel from Italy to Modane in France is an outstanding feat of engineering audacity and constructional skill by the Frenchmen who built it in the 1970s.

Bang in the middle of the tunnel is one of the world's most high-tech laboratories, built to conduct scientific experiments away from the prying eyes of cosmic rays. The trouble with cosmic rays is that they interfere with the study of proton decay, a subject high on the agenda of the modern nuclear-physicist The roof of this laboratory is made of six thousand feet of solid rock, which, I was not surprised to learn, reduces the muon flux, by a factor of a million. It is thanks to this laboratory that we know so much about spontaneous pion emission and even about dark matter. We may not be yet clever enough yet to put a foreigner on the right train, but we are exceptionally knowledgeable on the subject of double-beta decay.

I knew that the tunnel was nearly nine miles long and over ten yards wide. I was not too happy with the thought of those six thousand feet of rock arching over my head. To distract myself on the bus going through, I tried mentally to calculate the volume of rock removed in cubic yards. Whenever I was near an answer I would lose my decimal point, or forget whether I was working in imperial or metric units. I never reached an answer but this pointless calculation did not seem to matter much by the time there really was light at the end of the tunnel!

When I arrived at Modane, I was straining at the leash to start my walk as soon as possible, but first I had to do some shopping. I stocked up with two tins of sardines, a ripe cantaloupe melon, a chunk of local cheese and a French loaf, which would should see me through most emergencies.

The previous year in France I had found my mobile phone-bill expensive. My children, who intuitively know so much more about matters electronic than I do, had told me it would be cheaper to buy a French sim card to replace the existing card in my phone. By that simple trick, apparently, I would pay internal and not external rates for telephone calls to a Refuge just a few miles down the road. As instructed, I bought a French sim card, but my English phone was either too smart or too xenophobic to accept a French implant and simply refused to work with it. For once, the telephone companies were a step ahead of my children. They had spotted a loophole which might benefit their customers and closed it.

'Never mind,' said the helpful salesman.

'You were prepared to buy a French sim card for 30 Euros, but I can sell you a whole, brand-new, French phone for a mere 40 Euros.'

Unable to dispute this in my stumbling French, I left the shop the proud owner of two phones, one English and one French, which should delight the French President if no-one else. The French phone proved useful on a couple of occasions (but certainly not on 40 Euros-worth of occasions) when I needed to ring ahead to reserve a bed. I was many miles into the mountains south of Modane before I realised I was the proud owner of a phone for which I did not know either the tariff or the number. Perhaps I should leave complicated electronic matters to my children after all.

At last, just a couple of hours behind my original plan, I left Modane at 10 a.m. and for the next seven hours I climbed. This was not the ideal, break-yourself-in-gently stage I would have preferred for my first day. To compound matters there was a clear blue sky, a strong sun and no wind. I decided to plod slowly and stop whenever I wanted to, without setting myself any challenges or time targets. The gradient was severe at first. Coming up through the pine forest I saw no signs of the ancient track-ways carefully engineered for the passage of loaded pack-horses. An angry, latter-day Tourism Officer had set out these paths in revenge on people with the impertinence to leave his beloved Maurienne. There was n'ere a zig nor a zag in sight, only a path that went straight and mercilessly up the shoulder of the hill. So I trudged slowly upwards, chanting mantras like a Buddhist monk.

There were so many flowers of all shapes and in such a rainbow of colours that I was gradually distracted from the hardships of walking. My heart jumped with joy when I saw, for the first time, the alpine clematis. This, the original, indigenous European clematis, is more of a ground creeper in its natural setting than its exotic descendants that grow so luxuriously over the walls of nursery gardens. The flower of the original is a delicate pale blue and cream, and it droops so languidly and yet so prettily. Its pastel colours and graceful shapes reminded me of the art-nouveau illustrations in my much-loved childhood copy of *Peter Pan*. In my mind the alpine clematis will always be Tinkerbelle, the prettiest clematis of them all.

The GR5 has the good sense to by-pass Le Charmaix, a small ski resort closed for the summer. Despite my exasperation with ski resorts, I back-tracked through it because I particularly wanted to see the famous Chapel de Notre Dame, a medieval sanctuary consecrated to the Black Madonna. It sits, literally, between a rock and a hard place. Built against the wall of a ravine, it rests on the abutment of a high, narrow and delicate stone bridge designed for the passage of pack-horses and pilgrims. Since the chapel straddled their only route as they crossed the bridge, the pilgrims had little option but to pray, and give alms to the Black Madonna. It is an ingenious form of toll-church for pilgrims.

Black Madonnas abound throughout Europe and yet their origins are a mystery to scholars. Today people use them to bolster their own pet theory. Militant feminists welcome a strong female power in contrast to a pale-skinned, meek Mary of obedience and purity. Anthropologists identify pre-Christian links with Earth Mothers and Egyptian Goddesses. Modern theologians interpret them, somewhat conveniently, as reminders of the under-privileged black people of the world.

Today, it is just possible to glimpse the statue of the Madonna through the grille of the locked door. She is actually made of white marble painted black, but records show she was black in 1623 and the locals claim that their ancestors have venerated the Black Madonna here since the fourth century, although scholars think the Fourteenth Century to be more likely. I see the Black Madonna more simply as an illustration of that beautiful line in *Song of Songs* 1:5 – *'I am black, but beautiful, O daughters of Jerusalem.'*

I relished my first picnic lunch. Slices of juicy Cantaloupe melon and fresh chunks of bread with greedy portions of yellow-blue Termignon cheese left me in no doubt that I was back in France. During lunch I saw a most peculiar moth, about half an inch across. The normal moth part had mottled wings in pale buffs and browns, looking rather like a slice of cork. The abnormal part was two additional, small, black wings protruding from the front. It looked to me as if some sort of fly had had a high-speed, head-on collision with some sort of moth and in the impact they had become inextricably fused by their noses. Curious, I watched for several minutes but each set of wings seemed happy with its lot so I concluded that this was a natural state of affairs. I bought a book on insects when I reached Briançon but it failed to identify the creature to my satisfaction. The nearest I could guess was that it was a brindled beauty moth with a super-developed antennae. Except that this was June, and that particular moth flies only in April. This wonderland gets curiouser and curiouser.

Above the tree line, the going became easier and the path was better graded. The horizons moved backwards and upwards to open up a huge, primaeval landscape where streams and waterfalls fight their everlasting battles with rocks and cliffs. At last I was getting away from it all and into the real wilderness. I turned past a rocky corner and suddenly, to my amazement, I was on the Maginot Line. In front of me, a large concrete bunker straddled a small valley. Dark, grey and forbidding it looked as sinister and hostile as it must have done those seventy years ago when it was bristling with guns and manned by steel-helmeted soldiers. It was the incongruity of the situation that struck me more than the ugliness. Had there really ever been any sense in building such heavy concrete structures in such a remote spot? Obviously the French had once thought so. They had invested a great deal of money between the two world wars building defences on their mountain border with Italy. The bunker in front of me and the bigger emplacement that I could just see on the higher ground were just two small links of this long and highly ambitious chain of defence. I marvelled at the determination the French had shown in erecting such extensive buildings in such remote locations. The logistics must have been a nightmare in the age before the helicopter. Huge teams of pack-horses must have brought the cement and reinforcing steel up from Modane. Even if they found sand and gravel nearby, its transport would have required a huge amount of manual labour and yet more teams of pack-horses. Then the pack-horses had to be fed which required teams of ... and so on.

Unfortunately, all this valiant effort and great expense was to be of no use. The Italian Army did indeed attack across these mountain ranges in 1940, but only after the Allied resistance had been broken in the north and the French had insufficient troops to man their mountain Maginot Line and repel the invasion.

Although it was early summer there was still snow lying on the shoulder of Mont Thabor, and there were several snowfields to be crossed. Snow can be a hazard on the passes of the French Alps until as late as July. In the comfort of my home, I had persuaded myself that the route would not be sufficiently severe to bother with the hassle of carrying crampons and axes. I had pictured to myself the tantrums that airport security would throw at the sight of my ice-axe, which, in any case, is an awkward thing to carry around. Now that I could see the snow, I began to worry that I had made the wrong decision. On this first encounter the snow was slushy and slippery so that I found it difficult to keep my balance, but the going was level so a slip would mean nothing worse than a wet bottom. In fact the first snow, far from being dangerous, was great fun and I compressed handfuls of it into ice-cubes and dropped them down the back of my neck, where they melted between my shoulder blades. Ice-cold water trickling down my back was the nearest to ecstasy I would get that day.

The GR5 reaches the shoulder of Mont Thabor at the Col de la Vallée Etroite. Before the war this was the border with Italy, but today it is the boundary between the French Departments of La Savoie and Les Hautes-Alpes. Geographers consider it to be the demarcation point between the Northern and Southern Alps but none of that seemed of paramount importance to a walker flat on his back gasping to get his breath back

Eventually, on tired legs, I reached Refuge Mont Thabor at a height of about eight thousand, five hundred feet. The warden encouraged me to climb the last few feet of a snowfield by dancing like a dervish, whooping wildly and waving a bottle of beer in one hand, the other pointing to it. Apparently, the depth of snow on the passes had prevented him from opening the Refuge until two days before and I was his first guest of the season. Henri and I had a beer or two to celebrate.

I was spoilt for choice. I had forty-two beds to pick from, one pedal-flushed, high eco-value toilet of my own but no shower.

There was a problem, which I did not understand, with regard to water supply. Apparently there was enough water for cooking but not for washing.

'Never mind,' said Henri, 'the solution is simple. There is a lake just up the hill. It is good for washing.'

It had been a hot and sticky day, the sun was still warm and the prospect of swimming in the noddy in a remote mountain tarn seemed an attractive, if challenging, alternative to the usual semi-warm, spluttering shower in a cramped cubicle. Off I tramped with that day's washing, some soap-powder and my amazing, quick-drying towel under my arm. I walked over the ridge straight into the Arctic Circle. I could not initially see anything ahead that was not white. Against a background of white mountains merging into white cloud, was a flat sheet of ice several feet thick and covered in pure white snow. Lac Sainte Marguerite is certainly fresh; about half a mile square it had as much warmth in its welcome as my freezer. By the shore was one small area, about twenty yards square, of jet black water contrasting with the white ice all around. Swim in that! This was some practical joke by Henri. There was absolutely no way that my brain could persuade my body to submerge itself into that black hole. Good for washing, indeed! Yet I had to get clean.

Memories of freezing cold bath nights washed over me. When I was a child, domestic hot water was not as easily come by as it is today. My grandmother would stand me in a tin bath with about six inches of tepid water. Then she would say.

'First of all I will wash you down, as far as possible. Then I will wash you up, as far as possible. Then you can wash possible.'

I decided to stand naked in that Arctic landscape in six inches of freezing cold water and give myself a 'Grandmother Wash'. Possible preferred to wait for a warm shower tomorrow. Whilst I stood there splashing and shouting, a golden eagle soared overhead to see what all the fuss was about then, with a disdainful flick of his wings, he cruised on in search of more tasty tit-bits.

Washing clothes was not easy either, possibly because a soap powder has yet to be invented which lathers north of the Arctic Circle. As I trudged back barefoot through the snow, I noticed that there were no other footprints between Lake and Refuge. Henri either had a secret water supply or he washed infrequently.

This was France, the washing facilities might have been a little primitive but the kitchen services at Refuge Mont Thabor certainly were not. The two of us sat down, four or five hours' journey by packhorse from anywhere in particular, to enjoy a first-class, four course dinner. We started with a French onion soup, thick and well-flavoured as it should be. The main course was roast, smoked pork on a bed of spaghetti dressed with a sauce of mushrooms and green olives. The local Beaufort cows on the flanks of the mountain below, had provided us with our cheese course; a Tomme de Savoie. For dessert we enjoyed unsweetened yoghourt with a gelée of redcurrants. The whole was washed down with a local red wine. Henri and I talked constantly as we ate, never lost for words despite my inadequate French. It became apparent that he had a boundless love of the mountains and an encyclopaedic knowledge of everything to do with them, particularly of the passes and climbs on Mont Thabor which soared above us. As the evening progressed, and the wine sank lower in the bottle, slow-moving and serious-faced Henri became more and more animated. He enthused over the skill of the helicopter pilots, he told anecdotes of grizzled men of the mountains, stories of hunting Barons and of champion long-distance skiers. Alas, my ability to understand French declined in rough proportion to the level of the wine in the bottle and most of the later stories became blurred. But we were men of the mountains; we enjoyed each other's company regardless.

It is no wonder Henri waxes lyrical over helicopter pilots. Only the services of a helicopter make possible the abundance of good food in the Refuge. Three times a week it brings in fresh food and takes away the rubbish. The economics of this air-lift are a mystery to me. The costs must be sky-high and yet the charges to guests are trifling. Henri runs a superb establishment, without it the traverse of the GR5 and various other long-distance walks and local climbs would be nigh on impossible. I really hope that the accounts balance over the season and that the hospitality continues. At the same time, I do worry how one suave, athletic Englishman in sandals will be caricatured in Henri's anecdotes to tomorrow's visitors.

Chapter Fifteen

A Nutcracker at Last

Nowhere on earth was more beautiful than Mont Thabor that next morning. Henri and I appeared to have the planet to ourselves at the centre of a great amphitheatre of mountains sweeping beneath a clear blue sky. I breakfasted on a balcony cantilevered out into space, surrounded by the most magnificent vista. With a horizon in some directions of a few miles and in others of perhaps twenty miles there was no visible evidence, apart from the Refuge, that man had ever visited this area. This primaeval landscape absorbed my attention so totally that I did not notice I was unwashed, and I hardly cared that my breakfast was bread with no jam nor butter, washed down by coffee with no milk nor sugar. What more could I want in a panorama like this? What more could I need or expect in a place where a helicopter brings in everything?

I left the Refuge looking like the witless scarecrow from the Wizard of Oz. There had been a rainstorm in the night and my laundry was still damp. I had a variety of items of soggy clothing pinned and strapped to various parts of my rucksack; all blowing in the wind, flapping my farewells to Henri.

The flowers commandeered my attention from the moment I started to walk. I had collected interesting specimens all the previous day and had put them in my shirt-pocket so that I could identify them later from my trusty copy of *Fleurs des Alpes*. Preoccupied with the problems of Arctic ablutions, I had washed my shirt and forgotten all about the flowers in the pocket. My carefully-selected specimens were now a wet, congealed splodge and my botanical studies would have to start from Grade 1 again.

I had walked for an hour from the Refuge before I came upon a mountain stream with enough running water to wash in. Brushing my teeth, stripped to the waist in the chilly morning air reminded me of the Anapurna Circuit in Nepal. Known as the Andrex-Trail, personal hygiene in this primitive area creates something of a problem for public health. On the Circuit everyone leaves their overnight accommodation as soon as possible in order to find the first stream to perform their toilet. As a result, the first stream outside every village is a paper-decorated health hazard. There are no problems like that on the GR5 and that morning it was exhilarating to wash in a small waterfall, knowing that I would leave no trace. I baulked at shaving in cold water without a mirror and, as in Nepal, I resolved to grow a beard until I had hot water.

When I came down from the tops towards the tree line I saw junipers, low-lying and healthy-looking, for the first time on this walk. Among the junipers were swallow-tail butterflies. Two exotic, cream and black specimens were having a dog-fight, at great speed and with highly advanced aeronautical skills. I have never seen a swallow-tail in England so whenever I see the beauties on the Continent I watch them closely, but these two swooped and looped so quickly over such a wide area it was difficult to keep a close eye on them.

Thoreau said, 'Happiness is like a butterfly; the more you chase it the more it will elude you, but if you turn you attention to other things it will come and sit softly on your shoulder.'

I turned my attention to a cock ring ouzel flicking around some nearby rocks. Occasionally I see this bib-fronted thrush on the Yorkshire Moors. It is surprisingly shy for its size; which is not the norm in Yorkshire. Here, while I watched it going about its business, my happiness never left me and those swallowtails never found my shoulder. So much for Thoreau.

The larch forest was still green and fresh in early summer and at the higher levels the trees were sparse, opening up the opportunity for many colourful shrubs and plants to thrive. I walked in a day-dream in this idyllic scenery, fascinated by the three-dimensional movement of shadows created when trees are gently swaying in a breeze which at the same time is rippling the undergrowth. I was reminded of tall sailing-ships rolling and pitching in a gentle swell. Then I saw them. A roe deer doe was suckling her calf not twenty yards from me, clearly visible and highlighted by the sun in an open clearing. The calf was totally absorbed in his task and blissfully uninterested in anything beyond his food supply. The doe was very much aware of me, but she was not going to desert her young. Bravely she faced me; wide-eyed, probably petrified yet totally still. I watched them for only a few nano-seconds before I walked on quietly and quickly.

The descent from Mont Thabor to the Valley Etroite is defined by dominant mountain ranges on either side, both running approximately north-south. To the west are the French mountains of La Rocher Blanc and its flankers. On the east side, the Pointes Balthazar, Melchior and Gaspard guard the Italian-French border. I was surprised to meet the three wise men so much further west than has yet been reported. I thought that the Magi were Zoroastrians who went home to Persia by another way. Quite how they got this far west, knocking at the very gates of France, is a mystery. Zoroastrians worship the sun, so they are well-placed to oversee its setting in France every day. The three distinct Pointes had smaller peaks between them; humps which, when carefully examined, were clearly recognisable as the petrified remains of camels.

The first settlement of the day, Les Granges, still thinks it is part of Italy even though it became incorporated into France at the end of the Second World War. The little hamlet has a direct road down the valley to Bardonecchia in Italy, and a tortuous road link to the Region Briançonnus in France. The signs on the footpath and the house signs in the village are all in Italian and everyone greeted me with an emphatic '*Buon giorno*'. Whatever the politicians may claim, geographically and culturally, I was in Italy, not France.

Mont Thabor is a fine sight looking back from the south. Great skirts of scree rise high above the surrounding ridges, holding high in the sky an enormous, snow-covered squat column of rock. The sheer verticality of the rock face for several hundred feet makes one think of the castle walls and keep of a gigantic Norman Castle.

Above and beyond Les Granges the bright larches give way to the darker, less graceful pines. It was in the pine forest that I won the sight I had yearned for throughout my first trip – a clear view of a nutcracker. I was so close to this most distinctive bird that I had no need of my binoculars to be confident of its identity. About the same size as a jay, it is less colourful, with a browny, speckled body, not dissimilar in colouring to a starling. Its most distinctive feature is its white bottom, sometimes delicately described by effete ornithologists as white under tail-coverts. The clinching recognition feature is the white fan lacing to its tail. When the bird is in flight both features are prominent. This prize specimen flashed past me several times, determined that I should recognise and record it.

The nutcracker is a clever bird. Like the squirrel, it hoards its food to help it through the winter. It is particularly fond of the seeds of the yellow pine, which it extracts from the cones with sharp blows of its beak, hence its name. Cramming a hundred or more seeds into a special pouch in its gullet, the nutcracker flies around the countryside hiding seeds in caches spread over of several miles. Not only is it one of the few birds smart enough to use its beak as a tool, it is the only bird to have evolved a pocket in its gullet and it is brainy enough to remember most of its hiding places even when they are hidden under snow. In those few caches which it forgets, the seeds germinate, so the nutcracker contributes incidentally to the expansion and dispersal of its staple food. Not bad for a simple black bird with a white bottom.

I was hot, sweaty and dusty when I turned a bend in the track to hear the welcome tinkle of running water ahead; a rare treat to be greatly relished in the mountains. Today it seemed that I would be lucky and could drink as much as I liked, in pleasant contrast to days walking on dry ridges rationing a scarce water supply. As I off-loaded my rucksack and sorted out my purification tablets I heard the sound of cowbells. How idyllic! How melodic! The sounds were quite close and just above me. Oh no, they were directly above me! The cows were in the very ravine cut out by the stream that I was about to drink from. Tinkling took on a whole new meaning. I looked at the size of my tiny purification tablet and thought of the size of a cowpat. Deciding that it was an unequal contest, I repacked an empty water-bottle and resigned myself to a dry afternoon.

I was within a few of miles of my destination and there, clearly visible only two miles to the east, was Bardonechia where I had stayed the night before last. It had taken me nearly two days to walk back across the mountains that I had bussed under in less than twenty minutes. I could have hitch-hiked from there to here, but what would have been the point? I had enjoyed fourteen hours of world-class walking; infinitely more rewarding than twenty minutes in semi-darkness straining my brain with mental arithmetic.

On the edge of the small road that runs up to the border was a roadside chapel which had a foot in both countries, spiritually if not politically. The Chapel of Notre Dame de Bon Rencontre is little bigger than a pantry and yet it was overflowing with sprays of flowers, and with recent offerings, thank-you notes and petitions. Mostly they were prayers of supplication, as many in Italian as in French. Simple children's pictures accompanied some, while others were embellished with drawings of almost professional quality. The place was crammed full of paper prayers, as if it was some kind of sorting office between heaven and earth. The site has a further significance to many local people. Beside the Chapel there is a gilt-marble tablet installed in the 1990s to commemorate the fiftieth anniversary of the triumph of the French Resistance in the area. Today, at least sixty years after the events, there was a simple bunch of fresh flowers on that slab. Those flowers really got to me; somebody still cared, somebody was still in pain. Sixty years is nigh on three generations and the presence of those fresh flowers was not only a demonstration of love and strong family bonds but also a defiant shriek for human kindness in the brutal wilderness. I stood head-bowed for a brief while before those flowers, moved by many emotions – not least, deep compassion for whoever had laid them there.

Plampinet has not seen a builder these last hundred years, not for construction and certainly not for maintenance. The buildings are of a rugged, un-coursed stone, sometimes rendered in creams or greys, which support bleached, wooden shingle roofs, with only the occasional rusted corrugated iron sheet as a counterpoint. Overall, the village has a weathered and rather battered, please-leave-me-alone appearance which I found charming.

The leave-me-alone attitude was a distinctive feature of the village inn. I had difficulty gaining admission. He was engrossed in the repair of a rotovator while she was busy hoeing a small vegetable plot. They were far more interested in their horticultural sideline than they were in mine-hosting and it was some time before she could drag herself away to attend to me. She gave me a beer, showed me my room and went straight back to her vegetable plot. If there was a smile, I was not quick enough to notice it. The room was less than basic for the twenty-first century but, to me, it was luxury compared to the previous night's accommodation. The Inn must have some plus points, but a warm welcome was not one of them. So I drank my beer and told myself to be thankful for a warm shower and the opportunity to shave and to wash.

My fellow-guests at the Inn were a group of six workers from the local Electricity Company. They competed with the hosts for medals in cold-shouldering as an art form. How is it that the French can be more insular than the English who live on an island? My French is not fluent, but it is normally sufficient to engage with a Frenchman who is prepared to make a modest effort. After all, I had conversed with Henri for several hours last night. I tried different gambits to open up conversation with various Electric Men. A monosyllabic grunt rewarded every attempt; talking to me was too difficult, so they turned their backs and got on with their group rapport. They would probably be horrified to realise how such passive behaviour is so actively rude. Some Frenchmen are so Franco-centric that they cannot relate to anything that is not French; they buy French cars, never travel abroad and lead insular lives. Fortunately, there are more than enough open-hearted Frenchmen to make travelling in France enjoyable, but there were none in Plampinet that night.

The meal compensated for other shortcomings. The starter was a hot cheese and tomato flan on a huge bed of well-dressed salad. Mains, as the Americans say, was rare roast beef in a gravy rich with herbs and served with mashed potatoes twined with cheese. The crème caramel dessert was unremarkable but the complimentary liqueur was a delight; Liqueur de Genepi. This, for me, was a most appropriate finale; genepi is a small silver plant with yellow flowers found in the high pastures of the mountains and is the base of Chartreuse, that most holy of holy of all the liqueurs.

Cheered by the Genepi, I had another look round the village. In a more appreciative frame of mind, I found some interesting aspects. One of the most distinctive architectural features peculiar to this corner of France is the wall-sundial, the *cadran solaire*. It is a centuries-old art-form with a great variety of styles from every period, as artists of all schools have commandeered appropriate south facing walls on churches, town-halls and houses. They have painted the dials and surrounded them with cartouches on a grand scale and with astonishing exuberance and variety of embellishment. Here there are scrolls of clouds bearing puffing putti, over there is a geometric map of the heavens. What an attractive concept of public art, both practical and beautiful. Invariably there is included a motto about the passing of time, which inevitably lead to thoughts of death.

The motto on the sun-dial on the wall of the church at Plampinet amused me: 'If you knew this was your last hour you would not go fishing'.

For me that is undoubtedly true; even if I knew this was my last decade on earth, I would not go fishing.

I noticed that the predominant roofing material was wooden shingles. Mont Thubron is a watershed between different roofing practises. To the north the tradition for roofs of enormous stone slabs, locally called lauzes. Here to the south, the wooden shingle roof predominates. Both are extremely attractive in their setting and contribute greatly to a wide variety of very distinctive vernacular styles. Except where tin has invaded. In too many places, roofs repaired with sheets of corrugated iron spoil the look. Their use was understandable when times were hard and property values were low. In these prosperous times, fixing metal roofing on old buildings is a crime against the landscape. Frenchmen should unite against the Philistines, raise the tricolour, storm the barricades of tin-sheet factories and defend the true values of their Republic.

Chapter Sixteen

Use Your Brains, Not Your Backside

The Electric Men were smoking for France. When I came down to breakfast, the six were sitting in the small bar having their coffee and their cigarette smoke was thicker than an old London smog. I indicated to Madame that I did not like the smoke and that I would prefer to take my breakfast in the dining-room next door.

'*Pas possible*,' she said with the arms-folded, bonhomie of a Sumo wrestler, 'breakfast is served here, not there.'

It was a stand-off. I would not breakfast in the bar; she would not serve breakfast in the next room. I had settled my bill the night before so I asked for a refund.

'*Pas possible*,' she replied.

Impasse. Apparently I must have breakfast on her terms or not at all. We glared at each other across an invisible barrier of misunderstanding and suspicion caused by some small difference in cultural attitudes and hugely exaggerated by the lack of a common language (a state of affairs which has frequently led to war between our nations). Well, so be it. I knew a principle when

I saw one. St George did not back off when the dragon breathed smoke! With mounting aggression and pomposity, I decided to up the stakes and call in the law.

'Where is the Gendarmerie?' I asked.

She looked at me incredulously. It was a blatantly stupid question in a village of twenty houses, miles from any town. It broke the tension. We both burst out laughing. My breakfast was served in the dining room.

The best way to get from Plampinet to Briançon is to hire a canoe and paddle. The River Clarée runs through the village and on down the valley to join the River Durance just before Briançon. Failing a canoe, there is a pleasant and level walk alongside the river. The GR5 of course ignores such pleasant options. The GR5 does not do level, instead it climbs around the back of the high ridge of Pece defining the east of the Clarée Valley to the Col de la Lauze; a four thousand feet climb just for the fun of it. My limb and lung machines were moving towards synchronisation. I managed to climb the first thousand feet without stopping, something I emphatically could not have achieved on the previous two days. The landscape round the back of the Pece ridge is well worth the climb, with spectacular views of high scree slopes sweeping up to a long ridge of cliffs.

This is typical alpine chough country. A member of the crow family, the chough is shiny, jet-black and, although about the size of a jackdaw, it is infinitely more stylish; it is something a dandy with its delicate pale yellow beak and slim body. At this time of year they gather in small family groups of from three to six birds. For the choughs, the breeding season is almost over and they are about to launch their offspring into independence. I thought how well organised they were, particularly compared with the cuckoos that still could be heard plaintively calling from all along the tree line in belated attempts to find a mate and hopefully to begin the breeding process. Maybe not so belated – since the male cuckoo invests so little in the creation of his offspring those calling cuckoos could have been scoring breeding successes every day for the last three months. Perhaps the calls were less plaintive, and more exhausted.

As I climbed the last few hundred feet to the col a large ridge of wind-blown snow barred my progress. The wind had sculpted the barrier into a semi-circular cross-section, like a commercial greenhouse tube perhaps ten feet high and thirty feet across. I knew that when I got to the top of that ridge, without crampons or ice-axe, I would lose my balance and slide down the far side of the snow. Since the snow stretched across the path for about half a mile in either direction on a steep, grassy slope a detour was equally hazardous. So I walked up the hill, parallel to the ridge, looking for a safe-landing spot on the other side where the gradient would give me a fair chance of stopping my slide before it was too late.

Having chosen my spot, I climbed onto the ridge, gained the top and the inevitable happened. I slipped and skidded off the snow on my backside and I was fifteen yards down that treacherous, grassy slope before I managed to stop myself. I was lucky to have stopped without a cut, a bruise or something very much worse.

What a dangerous activity. No, what a stupid activity! I sat there recovering from the shock of the slide. I was angry with myself. Never, ever take a step knowing you are going to slip. Never, ever! Use your brains not your backside. Looking back, I worked out what I should have done. I should have taken my rucksack off and left it beside the track, to have better control of my balance. Then I should have knelt on the snow and with my bare hands, shovelled out a horizontal ledge across the ridge. Crawling across the ledge, as my shovelling progressed, my knees would have consolidated the snow beneath me. When I had cut a path right across the ridge then I could have crawled back and collected my rucksack. Certainly, I would have been wet and cold but intact.

There is absolutely no sense in knowingly taking any risk whatsoever, eight thousand feet up a mountain and alone.

Emphatically not, when there is the large, ominous black silhouette of a bird of prey circling overhead. I watched this sinister harbinger of doom watching me as it went round and round, waiting for me to fall. I took very careful note of the shape of its tail and recognised that it was an eagle, not a vulture; at least my eyes and other sensitive bits were safe for the time being. Those German geometry lessons had come in useful earlier than I had expected.

Beside the path were two mouse-skins. Flat, bleached and eyeless they were not pretty, but how, I wondered, did they get there? Presumably, a bird of prey with a big gullet had swallowed them whole. The rib cages were crushed on the way to the stomach, where the digestive acids dissolved all the soft tissues. I shuddered to think where, in this process, the poor creatures had lost consciousness. Once sucked clean of everything nutritious, the indigestible skin and bones were regurgitated and the poor creatures were literally hung out to dry. The most likely perpetrator of such a foul deed was an eagle owl, a monstrous flying killer twice the size of our barn owl. Normally, lunch for an eagle owl is a hare or a partridge, so two mice must have been his elevenses. He is so large and unopposed, so high up the pyramid of life, that he is one of the very few creatures in the mountains that can expect to die of rheumatism and old age.

Montgenèvre is a small remnant of an ancient hill village buried under an avalanche of modern ski-resort development. It is getting worse by the day. As I walked in, there were earth-moving machines and huge lorries working to level the next umpteen hectares for development. The only redeeming feature of this building site was the Grail Restaurant, which served a good lunch. The tables are set beside a nondescript French D road today. Yet at this very spot, as a paparazzi with a time machine, I could have photographed the Emperors Julius Caesar, Charlemagne, Charles VIII and Napoleon Bonaparte. Today's uninteresting D road is the historic military road used by Roman armies to subdue France, as well as for French armies invading Italy. Part of its military importance stems from this being the only pass in the French Alps open all winter. With the din and dust of modern machinery all around me I could get no feel for past glories. It is hard to imagine the tramp of foot-soldiers when a forty-ton truck is crashing by. The whole world quakes, the tables vibrate, the brain rattles in the skull and a cloud of dust dresses the salad. Visions of those four Emperors and the huge paraphernalia of their armies will have to wait until my next visit.

Montgenèvre was the leading French ski resort in the 1930s, favoured by that open pass, good snow cover on the slopes and long hours of sunshine. The resort had one of the first ski-lifts in the country. Badly damaged during the war, the place has never recovered its 1930 pre-eminence but it is now fighting to catch up, as those convoys of dump-trucks proved.

The village offered little to detain me and I decided to push on. At the Tourist Office before I left I had asked for a two-star hotel with a traditional French ambience in Briançon Old Town. They made a reservation for me at Auberge Valentin and assured me it met all my requirements.

The Topo Guide is the Randonneurs Bible. It gives the walker detailed route directions, good maps, charts showing the gradients of the ascents and descents, telephone numbers of remote gîtes and Refuges. Most helpfully of all, it gives the interval between places, not in kilometres, but in the hours it takes the average walker. Words like 'accuracy' and 'reliability' appear prominently in the mission statement of the Topo Guides. Until you get to Montgenèvre.

Since the Guide told me it was a walk of two hours down the hill to Briançon, I set off at 3 p.m. looking forward to arriving at 5 p.m. The Guide is wrong. The local signs indicated a time to Briançon of four hours, but I ignored them. What did the silly locals know in comparison to the wisdom of the Topo Guides? The answer turned out to be 'everything'. At 7 p.m. I walked into an Auberge in Briançon with my calf muscles almost locked solid in rebellion, after nearly twelve hours walking. Mostly the pain was in the mind. A projected four-hour walk that takes four hours is enjoyable; a two-hour walk that takes four hours is a nightmare.

There are some compensations for being a walker. Only walkers have the great privilege of arriving in Briançon by the grand Ashfeld Bridge. Crossing a deep and narrow chasm on the River Durance, this spectacular, single-span stone bridge crosses high above the boiling-white river. In the middle of the span a fine stone obelisk holds a cast-iron plate giving the history of the construction. General Ashfeld built it in 1734, with the military purpose of enabling supply convoys to move between the various fortifications around Briançon. In this wild setting of rocks, water and trees, at the centre of an outstanding feat of engineering, the obelisk itself is a work of art. It is let down by an intrusive and entirely unnecessary plastic plaque stating the obvious – 'This is a historic monument'. Any Epsilon semi-moron should realise that the monument would be even more historic without that superfluous, plastic intrusion.

Auberge Valentin turned out to be a hotel in the New Town and not the Old Town. Since an Englishman ran it, its French ambience was not immediately apparent. Tourist Offices do not usually get things that wrong. On this particular day it could not have been less French, as it was hosting the young ex-pat community. The Union Jack Bar was full of young Englishmen drinking beer and shouting in support of England playing World Cup football against Trinidad. I left them to it and went upstairs to soak my leg muscles in a hot bath. When I went back to the bar I found that I had missed 75 minutes of the match. Little had changed; there was no score and the fans were shouting louder as they unhappily contemplated a goalless draw. The English team must have sensed that I was bathed, scented, coiffured and ready because, in the dying minutes of the game, they scored two goals. The Engerländers went home quietly, more in relief than in triumph and I stayed talking with Brian at the bar. A big, burly blond, Brian is an English builder who earns his living from the ex-pat community in the area.

'It is too cold to mix cement when it is snowing between October and April, so I go home to see my mates. And my Mum,' he added as an afterthought.

'So you work here all the summer?'

'Well, not exactly. The Council don't allow building work in the Old Town in the high tourist months of July and August.'

'So you earn your living in May, June and September?'

'*Más o menos.*' He shrugged, lurching into Spanish. '*C'est un vie difficule, n'est ce pas?*' He winked. Having flaunted his fine linguisic skills in an unabashed Liverpudlian accent, he concentrated on his ninth pint of beer.

There are, he told me, some seventy Brits (his word, I hate it!) in Briançon, mostly young men employed in various local adventure-sport activities.

With the departure of the Engerländers I spoke to four leathered, latter-day Hell's Angels from Switzerland, hoping to recapture some of that missing French ambience. They were German-speaking Swiss and so naturally they had charming continental manners and spoke impeccable English. Frenchness was to prove elusive that evening – my quest would have to resume tomorrow.

Chapter Seventeen

It's Rude to Die on Tuesdays

Born of military necessity, fattened by trading opportunities and matured with political innovation, Briançon is a town with a distinctive story. This is not a town to rush through; it is unique in so many ways that it demands time from the traveller to savour and appreciate. I spent the day exploring. Its uniqueness stems from its unusual geography. Briançon has always been at the crossroads. Its location at the junction of five valleys at a critical point on the route between Arles and Milan gives it strategic importance. In Roman times, and probably for long before that, it was a military town. When the Romans withdrew, the local inhabitants carefully walled themselves in, on their rocky pinnacle above the Durance River, and waved to the rampaging Barbarians passing by below. In times of peace, a crossroads becomes a trading opportunity and by the Middle Ages the town had blossomed with many prosperous merchants. It became so wealthy that the town could afford to buy its independence from the Dauphine and establish itself as one of the first republics in post-classical Europe. By 1343 it was the leader of a confederation of five independent republics, called Ecartons, three of which were in present-day Italy and two in modern France.

This tiny island of a prosperous republic survived unnoticed and unchallenged in the huge ocean of European kingdoms for 400 years until the Treaty of Utrecht drastically re-drew the map of Western Europe, and indeed of the world. It was as if good Queen Anne had become impatient with the game of Monopoly, knocked the table over in a fit of petulance and then re-dealt the cards in her favour. England got great swathes of Canada from France and Gibraltar from Spain. Under the same Treaty, the Duke of Savoie became more powerful. He won Sicily and parts of Milan on the sole grounds that he was friendlier to the Austrians than he was to the French, and in the interests of some vague new concept, called the balance of power. In the general mayhem, nobody noticed that France snaffled the small, compensatory crumb of the Escarton of Briançon.

From that moment, Briançon was no longer a tiny republic forgotten in the mountains of beyond, she was a frontier town between France and Austria, on the firing line between the Bourbons and the Hapsburgs. From that day the military rather than the merchants held the mortgage on her future.

In 1690 the Duke of Savoie, Victor-Amadeus II, had proved his loyalty to the Austrians by invading France, and he came rampaging through the mountains. This put the wind up France, showing them that the mountains alone were insufficient defence. Imagining a threat from Austria and Italy (one that did not materialise until the modern era), the French set about modernising the ancient, medieval defensive positions. By 1740 the junctions of the five valleys were defended by five forts, some with linking bridges; a cornerstone of the French defences against the Austrians and later against the Italians The genius behind the work was Sebastian Vaubon who built a dazzling array of walls, gates, drawbridges, false brays and counterguards around the old town. The works survive to this day as some of the finest examples of eighteenth century defences in Europe.

The military were so dominant that they strangled any potential commercial development within the town. In reaction, the merchants breached Vaubon's walls from the inside and escaped to set up shop on the adjacent slopes to the south. The New Town (new in the eighteenth century) grew and evolved over time in response to economic pressures in the same way as any other town, whereas the Old Town stood still, locked in a time-warp by a military corset. As a result, the Old Town is a living museum and a great joy to visit. Narrow cobbled streets, flanked by colourful four-storey houses, lead up to a twin-domed church, complete, of course, with its *cadran solaire* on the front façade. There are two parallel streets running up the hill towards the church and both still have their original gargouilles.

The Old Town is in fact two forts; the later and more famous Vauban Citadel encircling an older fort rising in its midst In the older fort there are endless passages, staircases, tunnels, sentry boxes, walls and gateways to explore. On my visit I was alone with the birds keeping guard for me. Black redstarts were on sentry-go flitting from wall to wall with aerial patrols of swifts screaming overhead. The entire site is all the more interesting and inviting because it has an overgrown and unkempt feel to it. I wandered for hours amusing myself by trying to work out why this tower faced in that direction, why this and why that. I was happy, I was solving puzzles again. We do not have sites like this in England. As a member, I am a great admirer of the work done by English Heritage in the preservation of our historic sites. But I often ask myself if the grass really does need to be so well manicured. A castle courtyard never was a championship bowling green. Are so many barriers and safety notices really necessary? The sense of the magic and mystery of our past can be anesthetised by the presence of a steel banister rail to every old staircase, or a gaudy, plastic barrier to prevent access to anywhere remotely risky. I ambled freely around this old French castle and emerged, with not a twisted ankle or a grazed knee, but with both my curiosity and my interest well rewarded.

141

Paradoxically, for a place so unchanged by time, Briançon goes out of its way to record its passage. It is an al fresco art gallery of eighteen *cadrans solaires*. Finding some of them is of a challenge, but the most famous is the most obvious; the one on the front façade of the church in the main square.

Local aristocrats and merchants founded a Chapel of the Black Penitents here in the sixteenth century. There is nothing either black or penitential about their building; on the contrary, it is surprisingly cheerful with a tiled dome sitting on a square stone tower, all in perfect proportion. They needed a happy building to see them through their miserable work, that of consoling criminals condemned to death and providing burial services for the poor. The Black Penitents searched the town and collected all the corpses every Monday. Presumably, it was considered bad manners to die in Briançon on a Tuesday. Overall, I thought this was an impressive early form of efficient waste disposal. It reminded me of my local Council and its enthusiasm for complicated re-cycling programmes with different colour boxes and bins for different waste products to be collected on different days. When the Council tells me that it will collect black bags on Mondays, I will know that my days are numbered!

Not that it was Monday or that I felt like dying, but I decided to move on. A few miles from Briançon I found a gîte that pipped the Inn at Plampinet for the least welcoming welcome. Once again, Madame was weeding the front garden and we did our initial business right there without her straightening her back or pausing in her trowelling, nor even glancing in my direction. Short and veering towards the plump it would have been easier to talk to her face rather than her bottom.

'*Bon jour, Madame. Avez-vous un lit pour le nuit?*'

'*Oui,*' said the bottom.

'And will you serve a meal?'

'*Oui,*' said the, red-trousered derrière, like a robot.

I sat on the front step and waited. Half an hour later she managed to wrench herself away from her trowel, showed me my bunk, said that she would serve dinner at 7 p.m. and quickly went back to her weeding. Is that Franco-centric or just plain bad manners? But at least those red trousers bobbing up and down at the bottom of the garden like some giant pregnant robin digging for worms was a kind of human presence. In the next moment she had changed into her finery and, without a word, driven off, I knew not where. Alone, I felt like the only survivor on the Marie Celeste; I had a whole gîte to myself but no idea which parts were in bounds to visitors and which parts were not. After my reception at Plampinet, I began to feel a little depressed at the prospect of walking on my own for a couple of weeks if everyone was going to be so unforthcoming. Contented travelling, when there is little common language, depends upon smiling eye-contact and cheerful exchanges. That is a minimum. A little extrovert behaviour by either party helps break down reserve.

The arrival of Clickety-Clack interrupted my black thoughts. He came striding down the road bent forward from the waist, elbows jutting out, with walking poles taller than himself, clickety-clacking along at an impressive pace. He was wearing one of those Japanese-soldier caps with a large hanging flap to protect the back of the neck. The whole effect was a passable impression of an oriental, racing grasshopper. His achievements were certainly superhuman. He said he had come from Modane in two days, a distance I had covered in three days, and had been grateful for a rest day at Briançon to recuperate.

The Red Belgian arrived later. He rubbed more salt into my wounds with his impressive athletic prowess. He sported a fully-shaven head, was always smiling and I only ever saw him in a red vest and shorts. He was fluent in French and English – all too fluent. If I had been worried about the lack of conversation, I need worry no more. If you asked a question in one sentence, he replied with a chapter. No detail was withheld, the reply was complete with footnotes and appendices and often translated into a second language for the benefit of a wider audience. Under this verbal onslaught conversation withered. I re-christened him the Walkie-Talkie.

He was walking the GR5 in the opposite direction to me and had come from Nice in nine days. When he talked of sleeping in shepherd's huts and running up and down hills, I knew that we were in entirely different leagues athletically, and that my journey would take much longer.

Looking at these two champions of the GR5 I pondered the difference between them and me. Thirty years for a start, and probably three stone as well. But self-indulgence is the real answer. I can seldom resist the temptation of that second glass of wine, whereas probably they turn up their prim, ascetic noses at the first glass. They were below average height and each had a Body Mass Index veering towards the anorexic. I am above average height and at my annual health check, the nurse clucks the same chorus year after year.

'Tut-tut! You must try harder.'

Try harder? I am walking the GR5, for goodness sake!

Chapter Eighteen

Great-grandmother Rules

The Gents' Outfitter in Nice is an eleven day march from the Gents' Outfitter in Briançon, and there is nothing even vaguely similar in between. This may be of little interest to the world until now, but it became of seismic importance to me. Be warned, if travelling along the GR5 with only two pairs of pants, do not lose any. Yes, I realised too late that I had left a pair hanging on the line last night and that I had a very long hike to Nice in front of me. It would have to be a simple 'one day off, one day on' routine. Since I was walking in shorts I would need to be careful on the 'off' days and hope that I did not meet too many inquisitive and biting insects.

I am not a novice in the art of walking in the altogether; I have previous form. My wife and I were once hitch-hiking around the jungles of Borneo. On one occasion, we were travelling with just the clothes we stood up in when we got soaked in a tropical rainstorm, which also washed away the bridges. We had a ten mile walk along a jungle track before we had any chance of meeting a vehicle. After the storm, it seemed a bright idea to take all my dripping clothes off and let them dry flapping from my rucksack as we walked in the sunshine. After all there was nobody about. I was some way ahead of my wife when a man materialised from nowhere. Tall and muscular, wearing only a loincloth, he carried a long blow-pipe with a quiver of evil-looking darts. He took a good look at me from top to bottom and spoke cheerfully in his own tongue.

I think he probably said: 'Good morning, Sir. You must be a chief where you come from!'

My wife was approaching and before I could reply, he disappeared as instantaneously as he had appeared. Obviously a clothed Englishwoman was far more embarrassing to him than a naked Englishman.

My wife thinks he probably said: 'Oh dear me! You are too skinny to be worth cooking.'

Naked or not, there is a consistency to walking the GR5. Almost every morning demands a painful and laborious climb of about four thousand feet to the ridge and every afternoon provides a blissful descent, wondering what all the fuss was about. The path usually starts in the dense and tedious pine forest. Nothing much grows or lives beneath thick canopy. There is nothing to distract one, and nothing to think about except the mind-numbing business of getting the body into gear and picking the easiest footfall through the rocks and roots. Gradually, as the path climbs, the forest thins out and gives way to the lower alpine pastures. Here there are flowers and butterflies and birds, even the occasional mammal, to distract the mind. At last, sharp crags of the mountain ridges and peaks begin to appear above the trees in various directions. Increasingly there is more to see and the landscape becomes grander with every step. Yet these pleasures demand their price; by now the lungs are straining, the knees are screaming, even though the soul is in countdown to lift-off. Imperceptibly, the pines fade away, replaced for a while by ground-hugging junipers. At the tree line, the soul soars triumphantly; there are mountain peaks on every horizon: huge, sheer cliffs of rock; vast, steep-angled boulder screes, ridges of incredible serrations and sharpness. The mountains are magnificent; they are worth every penny of the pain needed to gain admission.

Then suddenly it is all over. I have reached the ridge. I throw off my rucksack. My soul is now in free orbit. There, far below and barely visible, is tonight's village. Facing across the valley is another range of mountains; another set of ridges with cliffs and screes looking higher and even less surmountable than today's ridge looked yesterday. Tomorrow's route seems impossible without oxygen cylinders or donkeys, or preferably both. But I'll think of that tomorrow. I have decided to dedicate the rest of the day to full-time hedonism.

Men have been crossing these cols for millennia. In the Iron Age, travel would have been difficult through the valleys because of the swampy woodlands and unfordable rivers. Often it would have been too dangerous because of the nasty men lurking in the undergrowth. So early man had to find his way across the ridges, often accompanied by his family and, in the time before domesticated animals, carrying all their needs. For these reasons, you can be sure that the paths above the tree line are the best line of climb for that particular terrain; they are the distillation of the experience of hundreds of generation of foot-weary humans. Below the tree line it is a different story. The prehistoric tracks have long been obliterated by centuries of neglect and by forest growth. Modern man made the existing tracks in the forest, driven by commerce and assisted by machines. Forestry is the commercial force which creates tracks in the uplands today, but tracks designed for loaded timber-tractors are useless to walkers. Crudely bull-dozed, ugly scars, axle-deep in slurry; forestry tracks coil up the mountain at a gradient which gives too lazy a rate of climb for the walker. So modern, tourist-officer man has sign-posted footpaths which cut off the loops of the forestry tracks, but these are often too steep for comfortable walking up or down.

Sometimes the tracks developed before the steam age happily have a use again. Mining, in the old days, depended upon pack-horses. Their tracks are pitched to a gradient that is ideal for the modern walker and they are often still well surfaced; romantic reminders of a passed era. Walking them, as they weave through the woodland on the lower slopes, it is often possible to visualise a string of ponies struggling along the path. For some reason, I always picture their driver wearing a bright red bandana, gold earrings and swearing profusely.

At the top of the Col de Ayes there was another snowfield blocking the path. This one had a thirty-foot drop on the far side and was a dangerous prospect in sandals and without an ice-axe. Fortunately, it could be by-passed by a careful scramble on my backside down a wet slate, scree slope. I had long given up any expectation of clean shorts on this trip so I moved very slowly, making sure that I always had three points of contact with the ground. I may have looked like an inverted crab with back-ache but I made it without mishap, albeit with wet and dirty shorts.

I had seen a couple of walkers coming up behind me and so I waited to see if I could help them over the hazard. Such is the camaraderie of the mountains. I need not have bothered – they were Dutch. Why do the Dutch always seem so at home in the mountains? Coming from a country without so much as a one-hundred-foot contour of its own, they cannot have evolved a mountain-climbing gene. Furthermore, they mostly seem to be excessively tall with the stride of a galloping giraffe. Presumably the answer is that the Dutch approach the alien environment, as they do everything, with a great deal of deliberation and application. These two had walking-poles and, coming up to the snowfield, they looked at the drop, saw where I had come across and followed, hardly breaking their stride. With their walking-poles to support them they simply walked across. No fuss, no hesitation. That was one of the few occasions, in walking hundreds of miles in French mountains, when I would have been better off with an ice-axe or walking-poles. To deny the Dutch any feeling of superiority, I broke into my Kinabalu Trot and was a thousand feet below them in no time. Such is the camaraderie of the mountains!

For three days I had walked with an unbroken blue sky. It had clouded over at Briançon and today it rained. Not a short, sharp thunderstorm, but steady rain with a cold wind. Out came my poncho, and I trudged along, dry inside but dripping at the edges.

The first impression on approaching the village of Brunissard was of the high proportion of shining tin roofs; surely an indication that, if there had ever been a pretty alpine village here, it would now be lost under a mudslide of new development. My fears were confirmed, although one or two attractive old buildings have survived, including, to my great good fortune, the Restaurant Chez Marius. The meal cost next to nothing and Marie served it with a smile. A plate piled with Parma ham and melon was followed by roast chicken, roast potatoes and vegetables. A tasty cheese course, a delicious chocolate mousse, demi-carafe of local wine and a cup of coffee brought the total cost to the equivalent of £10. At prices like this I could not afford to go home.

My original plan for the day had been to make the eight-hour trek to Chateau Queyras, which by now was only two hours' walk away. This is a settlement with its name printed in big, bold type on the map. The print is large enough to implant in the brain a distinct impression of hotels, bars, boulangeries, épiceries and all the other essential trappings of civilisation to be expected in a small French town (even, perhaps, a Gents' Outfitter). Marie told me that there were no facilities whatsoever to enjoy at Chateau Queyras and that the next bed on the GR5 was a further eight hours walk beyond.

There were not many options. It was two o'clock in the afternoon. There was a two-star Logi, fifteen minutes down the track or a gîte eight hours walk away in the rain. The Walkie-talkie may relish sleeping in a derelict hut on top of a mountain in the rain but I am made of softer stuff. I booked into the Logi at La Chalp.

149

It proved to be a four-star family-run hotel with four generations on hand. Not that great-grandmother did much other than petulantly, yet purposefully, bang her stick on the floor whenever somebody switched the giant TV screen over to the football channel. It was just as well that England was not playing that day; great-grandmother would have beaten me into pulp before half-time. The children, at three and five years old, offered kisses to guests and asked for their autograph, as good a start as any to creating a friendly atmosphere. The two intervening generations managed to provide a warm welcome, excellent clothes-drying facilities, clean rooms and a well-stocked bar, and with a smile at every turn.

I was not surprised to be served a superb, five-star, five-course meal. The additional course, served between the soup and the meat, made a distinctive impact on the meal. Bruyard is a delicious concoction made of eggs, mushrooms and cream. It is incredibly light; as far removed from an omelette as a meringue is from a dumpling. The mushrooms give it a sweet, herby flavour which belies their doom-laden name of Trumpets of Death. This was indeed a French family hotel at its best.

Chapter Nineteen

The Very Best of Eating

It was a drab, dreary morning. Rain was drizzling from a grey sky and the forecast was dismal. The next place to sleep was over nine hours walk ahead.

'Think positively!' I told myself at breakfast. I instructed myself to write down all the positive points of walking for a day under a dripping poncho. I failed miserably; after ten minutes I was still staring at a blank piece of paper, so I ordered a taxi. It dropped me off at Chateau Queyras leaving me with a mere seven hours walking in the rain.

Chateau Queyras is a dramatic edifice straight from a fairy tale; a walled castle isolated on a rocky outcrop. Yet another of my childish simplifications of French history died on that rock. I had always thought that all the French Kings were Catholic and anti-Protestant. Wrong. All were Catholic but some were tolerant and inclusive and sought to accommodate the Protestants; others were fundamentalist, exclusive and waged absolute war on Protestantism. A hundred years of bloody battle between Catholics and Protestants had its repercussions even in the remote

151

borderlands at Chateau Queyras. A dilapidated signboard at the castle gate gives the bare bones of the story. A General Lesdiguieres held the place in 1587 and a Count of Schomberg failed to take it by siege in 1692. Those two dates and events just about bracket the rise and the fall of the Protestants in France; they roughly coincide first with the proclamation and then with the revocation of the Edict of Nantes. At the outset of the saga, in 1587, General Lesdiguieres was a Protestant Royalist in the service of the Catholic King Henry IV. His mere appointment indicates a degree of religious tolerance at court. A brilliant soldier, he controlled the Dauphine, and he garrisoned Chateau Queyras to repulse the probing challenges of the Duke of Savoie, who was sniffing for opportunities at a time when the internal disputes of the religious factions were weakening France. The Edict of 1598 guaranteed (nearly equal) rights to Protestants and brought a measure of peace and unity to the land. The Edict is better known for its revocation in 1685, denying Protestants all rights and causing a wholesale exodus of large sections of the population from all over France. An own-goal for France, it was both a political and an economic disaster, handing the economic benefits of a huge influx of skilled Huguenot (Protestant) craftsmen and merchants to England, Germany and the Low Countries. At the time, there were witch-hunts all over the country to root out Protestants. Some of these were hiding in Chateau Queyras, where the Count of Schomberg tried unsuccessfully to flush them out.

The climb out of Queyras was much easier than usual. The gradient was slight as the path climbed, following a stream through the inevitable pinewoods to alpine pasture and finally to grand scree slopes. The rain spat a little but never became serious and so what had started as a dour day turned out to be thoroughly cheerful. A twinge of conscience asked whether I had taken the taxi under false pretences. Of course I had, but nobody need know. I tossed my conscience behind me and concentrated on the flowers.

My identification book sorts the plants according to the colour of the flowers. Most of the stunners are in the purple/blue section. There is no doubt for me that the most beautiful flower of all in the Alps is the gentian (*gentiane acaule*) with its large trumpet-shaped flowers and its unbelievably rich, blue-verging-to-the-purple colour, which I do not think has ever been matched in even the most sumptuous of man-made dyes. It grows above the tree line but the sight of a single flower itself makes the climb worthwhile. A good second choice is another gentian (*gentiane printaniere*). This is a much simpler flower than its cousin, with five-petals in child's-drawing simplicity, but the colour, slightly bluer, is just as rich. There are several fine campanulas which grow naturally in the Alps. *Campanula cochleanfolia* provides a fine spray of small, blue, bell-shaped flowers nodding in the breeze just a few inches above the ground. *Campanula scheuchzea* is slightly taller and more purple; a delicate and graceful plant. The indigenous aquilegia, (*aquilegia alpine*) is delicately coloured and so much finer than the cultured variants sold in nurseries. No commercial item matches the deep purple colour or the elegant display of fine petals and, of course, there is no garden on earth that can match the setting of a high alpine meadow. The simplest of the purple flowers is a pansy (*viola lutea*). It is large, several times larger than the English wild pansy, and it displays a single, two-dimensional flower-head of intense, unvaried purple. There are yellow variants but they lack the vibrancy of colour.

Having so enjoyed that liqueur at Plampinet I was always on the lookout for the genepi flower, *genepia mutellia*. It is an easily-missed spray of feathery, grey-green foliage with stalks of several very small yellow flowers. Generally, it prospers at high altitudes where it comes under the protection of National Park, which prohibits picking wild flowers. How is a poor, hard-done-by Frenchman to exercise his God-given right to make genepi if he cannot pick the flowers? This being France, where legislation is tempered by the will of the people, the unwritten rule is: 'You cannot pick any flowers – except for forty genepi'. Where are the Park Rangers to count the forty-first genepi? I rarely saw any on my travels.

Refreshed by the morning's taxi-ride, I thrashed the Topo Guide time predictions and arrived in Ceillac much earlier than expected. This gave me a choice; I could get another stage of the walk under my belt or I could have the afternoon off. Long-term planning was impossible anyway because I was about to walk off the edge of my map. Unless I could buy the next map, or Topo Guide, within a couple of days my precise navigation would degenerate into blind man's bluff. I had no idea if I was on schedule with the walk, simply because I did not have a schedule. My bookings allowed me seventeen days between flights at Nice, but I had never sat down to work out the journey. That would be too much like a plan, a suggestion of regimentation where none was necessary. If I arrived at Nice with days to spare, I could sunbathe on the beach, or even take some sun-tan lotion to Ventimiglia! If I ran out of time, I would come back and finish the walk over an autumn week-end. Both prospects were attractive, so why worry? I decided to spend the afternoon enjoying Ceillac.

The coffin of a giant sits at the entrance to the village. This large timber box some eight feet long by two feet wide and two feet deep, each side made from a single piece of timber two inches thick, is a tribute to the local craftsmen. Closer inspection revealed it to be full of water – not a coffin but a fish tank. A constant stream of water splashed noisily into a bubbling, short compartment then calmly slipped over into a second, long and tranquil compartment. Placidly swimming around this lower section were five fine river trout, each about a foot long. I could not find out who owned them. Perhaps they were just a hint to the traveller that this was a village not only with a high standard of cuisine but also a low level of crime.

Ciellac may be a small village but it has grand pretensions. There are four or five civic fountains at various strategic points, all built to the same design. A central tower has four spouts at right angles to each other, spilling water into one large, circular basin. Some are made carved from wood, some sculpted in stone and most have elaborate, decorative spouts; all are in good working order.

I had never seen a semi-detached church before, nor one that is also L-shaped with a built-in bell-tower. St Sebastien is a church with a difference and I was intrigued. The larger nave has a light pink render outside and inevitably is home to a *cadran solaire*. This one has been telling the time of day since 1732. At the junction of the two naves is not the usual stone tower, instead there is a bell-wall; a high stone wall projecting well above the roofs, pierced at irregular intervals by six holes each housing a weighty bronze bell. The wall is capped by a huge timber roof cantilevered up and out from the wall; a most unusual structure to dominate a village square. I entered the building through the Romanesque stone arch to discover that I was in a church of two halves. The main leg is the large nave of the parish church, capped by a vaulted stone roof set to a gothic section, whereas the foot of the L is another nave housing a Penitent's Chapel with its own external entrance. I warmed to its harmony and attributed its unconformity to the free spirits of the mountains.

Wood-carving is a traditional craft in all the villages of the Alps and at Ceillac they make a business of it. They carve deep floral patterns from the slow-growing yellow pine; the nutcracker's friend. Every conceivable domestic object was available in carved pine; salt boxes, table lamps, cupboard doors, butter-dishes; the list was endless. I dare say I could have ordered a working vacuum-cleaner in carved pine. To emphasise its tradition the village has a distinctive sculpture; a larger-than-life wooden statue, carved from a single piece of wood and labelled the 'Hiker'. It is a memory of a time when hikers wore large hob-nailed boots, baggy trousers, a waistcoat with a watch-chain, a heavy tweed jacket and a cloth-cap. I renamed it: 'Robert Louis Stevenson looking for his donkey'.

155

The sun finally came out in the late afternoon, opening up spectacular views of mountains in every direction. I spent some time carefully orientating my map so that I could identify each peak, but lost interest when a Golden Eagle paraglided overhead, seeming to be in slow-motion, its wing-feathers outstretched like the fingers of a beseeching hand. For as long as I could, I watched him gliding and soaring so effortlessly. He was the ultimate in flying machines. With no noticeable sign of exertion, he was over this hill at one moment and the other side of the valley the next. If only I could move through the mountains with no more effort than the occasional flick of a wing-feather.

Probably, Clickety-Clack felt the same. He came to the gîte that evening with the same mechanical, grasshopper movements, although this time he reminded me more of a mechanical toy with a run-down battery. He did not want a word of conversation and he clacked his way straight to bed, presumably to plug into his overnight battery-charger. He missed a good meal and the conviviality of the evening.

The Gîte d'Etape at Ceillac is an alpine Tardis. Seemingly small, that evening it was home to about twenty walkers, and fifty, late-teenage schoolchildren with their teachers. It promised to be a noisy night; I hoped Clickety-clack had ear-muffs. In the early evening we all sat together on the grassy banks outside. The youngsters entertained us to an impromptu, occasionally disjointed, yet highly talented, jazz concert with two guitars, a recorder and drums. They were full of fun and their enthusiasm was contagious; none of us on that grassy knoll had a care in the world. All the ingredients of my personal paradise were there –a warm setting sun, convivial company, a cold beer, laughing youngsters, strains of jazz and panoramic views of mountains. There was only one person missing, but hopefully the gardening would be up to date.

The *al fresco* music was the prelude to a distinctly Gallic evening! In the dining-room some eighty people sat down simultaneously to dinner at twelve tables. Immediately, cheerful young waitresses placed great tureens of pea and ham soup on each table. Everybody seemed to serve everybody else, nearly everybody had second helpings and yet the tureens went back with soup to spare. Next came large platters of lamb kebab and dishes of roast potatoes. Again, everybody was courteous in looking after their fellows, again second helpings were taken and still food was removed. Needless to say, there was more cheese and dressed salad than we could eat. Finally, chocolate mousse filled any few remaining empty spaces. After the meal everybody played their part in clearing and cleaning the tables before the grand finale of *'bon nuits'* and mass kissing on both cheeks. To enjoy the very best in communal eating, with good company, good manners and top value for money, simply find a busy Gîte d'Etape in France.

Chapter Twenty

Vive La Tomme Ubaye

There was no obvious way out of Ceillac to the south. The route seemed blocked by the massive bulk of the Pics de la Font Sancte, a sparkling range of mountains with tops over ten thousand feet and with large, year-round snowfields. These are the last roars of the royal lions of the Alps. After this the cubs take over and although the scenery is splendid, the great heights, the snowfields and the grandeur are lacking.

The path picks its way along the northern slopes of the ridge, first through the hanging valley of Ceillac and then up through larch forest to the Lac Miroir. A green lake, in an oval bowl of grassland, it reflects the violent ridge soaring above. My timing was perfect; there was no wind, the sun was bright and in the right position to show me a precise reflection; a happy coincidence of circumstances that might require a professional photographer to wait for several days.

The forest soon receded and with a scramble over rough scree I reached a second lake set in as magnificent a landscape as I had seen anywhere in the world; and I had it all to myself. Lac Sainte Anne is a deep aqua-marine pool, framed on the far side by a thrusting, jagged ridge of tumbling, grey rocks climbing up through crystal-white snowfields to a peak at eleven thousand feet. Miraculously there is a small Chapel, dedicated to Sainte Anne, beside the lake and I sat in its porch, overwhelmed by the grandeur of the scene, feeling like a miniscule micro-dot lost in a giga-galaxy.

I could have been the only living creature in the whole world and my insignificance in the wider scheme of things hit home hard. In the solitude my mind soared over thoughts of the creation and the purpose of the world; of the meaning of life. For me, with a deep suspicion of the supernatural explanation, there were no rational answers, only an endlessly spiralling tangle of more questions in my puny and futile efforts to separate reason and faith. The answers to philosophic questions always feel nearer to discovery in the magnificence of the high mountains than they ever did in the lecture-rooms of a University, although sometimes I have been close in my local Public Bar.

Since I had failed abjectly to answer any of the fundamental questions I reined my mind back from the supernatural to the natural, to the here and now. Even here in the land of the Gods my mind had to have reason. Why was one lake green and one lake blue? Was it to do with the refraction of light, or was it caused by the chemical composition of the water? Was it physics or chemistry? My reason had not got me very far when my reverie of thoughts was interrupted by the arrival of a large party of day-walkers and the peace of the scene was shattered. End of philosophical meditation, time to walk.

It was not a long walk to the Col Gerardin and there, once again, I had the world to myself and the world from there was beautiful. I was on a ledge, sandwiched between Peaks and I was on top of the very wall which had seemed impenetrable when I had looked across from the col yesterday. Today I sat at the top of a great bowl of rock sweeping down grandly three thousand feet to the Ubaye River below. I promised myself lunch on the banks of the river with my feet cooling in the water.

It is lightly trodden this GR5 and the path is not always easy to find. Not once, but three times, I was so eagerly scanning for the route ahead, that I walked into a clump of stinging nettles. That is a stupid thing to do at any time; it is particularly daft to do it on an off-day.

The path hit the valley bottom at the small hamlet of Le Barge. Most welcome of all, after several hours crossing a dry ridge, was the water running into a stone trough giving me the opportunity to fill the water bottle and add the chemical fizzers. Several large, stone-built farmhouses and barns were huddled together but there was no sign of any recent agricultural activity and the place was devoid of any human presence. I guessed that the redundant buildings were about to be redeveloped, probably as second homes. Given a choice between the slow crumbling decay of the buildings and their glitzy rebirth as holiday-lets I could just about stomach the change; providing there were no tin roofs! Lunch by the stream, in a grove of alders, with bare feet dabbling in the cold, running water was idyllic.

I noticed a hiker just off the road with his rucksack on the ground making adjustments to the strapping. I had not seen him before, so I guessed that he was walking the GR5 in the opposite direction to me. He was in his forties, fair-haired and lithely built; he gave off an aura of competence. '*Bonjour,*' I called over the ten metres of intervening grassland. He did not react so I raised my voice and called again. This time he responded and we exchanged the formalities. He had, indeed, walked from Nice and was now making for a village a few miles up the road. According to him I had a thirty-minute walk to Fouillouse. With the completion of this typical walkers' brief but friendly information-exchange, we said our farewells and I walked on. Immediately, I realised that he could tell me how many days walk we were from Nice. I walked back towards him across the grass verge.

'Monsieur,' I called from thirty yards.

He did not hear. I called again, more loudly, from twenty yards. No response. Unquestionably the man was hard of hearing. What should I do now? If I turned back and he saw me so close he would wonder what I was up to. I continued to advance slowly, shouting more and more loudly. Suddenly, when I was about ten yards away, he realised that I was there. He turned towards me, his face contorted with violent anger, his body crouched and his arms tensed in the aggressive posture of a street-fighter with a knife. 'Why are you there? Our talk is finished! Go! Go!'

He seemed to me dangerously out of control and I immediately backed off, keeping my face towards him and on my guard, saying 'I go. I go!'

I walked backwards not daring to let him out of my sight. It was an unpleasant moment. I realised, too late, that he was extremely deaf and I could not work out how he had managed to take part in the first conversation. Surely, he had not been able to lip-read my hesitant French. My unexpected return had caused him great alarm which had instantly changed into explosive anger. I was annoyed with myself for frightening the man.

With a hundred yards between us, still looking over my shoulder, my emotions turned into self-righteous indignation. If the man was so sensitive, so easily frightened that he became so dangerously aggressive, then he should not walk by himself.

Two hundred yards on I stopped looking over my shoulder continuously; the relative safety melted my indignation and I felt some sympathy. The man had problems enough being deaf; of course he should be free to walk the mountains. Four hundred yards on and I was generously wishing him a happy trip; but I still glanced back frequently.

This jewel of a day, when I walked for nine hours past emerald-coloured lakes and between diamond-tiara mountain ridges, finished at a tiny pearl; the hamlet of Fouillouse. How anyone got to the place in the old days was a puzzle to me, but today the road from the valley gets there across a small stone bridge, spanning crazily between vertical rock faces three hundred and twenty feet above the river. Big Ben could sit under that bridge and leave space to spare! It is such a distinguished and extravagant construction that I suspect the cost of building was justified more by the need to get gunpowder up to border defences rather than to take Fouillouse cheese down to market.

A giant overstatement of a building, the Gîte d'Etape at Fouillouse is a good example of an Ubaye farmhouse. It is massive both in its size and in the strength of its construction with three very large storeys rising from a ground floor wall strongly buttressed on all four sides. The ground level has a stone-vaulted ceiling with strong quartered arches allowing a great deal of weight to be stored above. There are hardly any window openings and the few that exist are metal-grilled and heavily shuttered. The roof, once timber-shingles but now corrugated iron, has a five-foot overhang, indicating that there is plenty of winter snow hereabouts. Great chunks of timber, about twice the section of railway sleepers, polished by the feet of generations, make an impressive staircase. The whole building would look like a prison were it not for the colourful parasols on the terrace.

I found it hard to imagine that farming was ever sufficiently profitable in these remote upland valleys to underwrite such costly buildings, which would be difficult to build in phases and require a combination of a heavy initial financing and total confidence in the future. Perhaps there was some earlier incarnation of the Common Agricultural Policy subsidising French agriculture one hundred and fifty years ago.

At least the gîte farmhouse has an economic use which will keep it maintained. That is, unfortunately, probably more than can be said for the rest of the village. There are another six, cavernous farmhouses in varying states of collapse. The roofs, long-since repaired in corrugated iron are now rusting through and within a few years will no longer serve their purpose. When that happens this village and similar, remote high-pasture settlements, will slowly wash away. The church is already in peril. The small nave with a simple bell-wall echoing that of Ceillac has served the village since 1579; now, with a minimal population, the Friends of Fouillouse are at their wits end to raise the money required for its preservation.

Napoleon and Josephine ran the Auberge Les Grange with great efficiency and full French charm. Napoleon managed the front of house. Short in stature, with a well-muscled frame he had a quiet air of command. His body language declared 'This is my hotel and I am in charge'. Everything was calmly organized; the dos and don'ts were set out in amusing cartoons on the walls wherever necessary. Mine host unquestionably could write the Napoleonic Code for Hoteliers de France. Josephine controlled her side of the house with an entirely different technique – her flouncing flirtatiousness would be coquettish in anyone other than a French woman. I was happy to be in their capable hands.

I shared my dining table with the Three Musketeers; middle-aged Frenchman on holiday, travelling by car with just a token amount of walking thrown in. Aremis, Porthos and Athos swashbuckled through the meal with me as their bemused d'Artagnan. Nothing said by the one could pass without witty riposte from the others. They certainly knew their mountains. Over the dinner they mentally retraced my footsteps from the shores of Lake Geneva to Fouillouse. None of them had actually walked the GR5 but over the years obviously they had walked all over the French Alps. Without recourse to a map, between them, they could name every col, every valley and every village that I had walked on the route. In spite of our language problems we bonded over that discussion on mountains and d'Artagnan became a musketeer, at least in spirit.

The cheese was clearly something special. Napoleon produced it with a theatrical flourish to show me that I was in for a significant gastronomic experience. After a military briefing between Napoleon and the Musketeers, they decided to grant me

163

the privilege of tasting the local cheese. For a foreigner to be awarded the Ubaye Tomme is not quite as distinctive as receiving the Croix de Geurre, but it is close. Surrounded by proud, expectant faces I took a mouthful. It was a non-event. I made great, lip-smacking sounds of enthusiastic appreciation, but it was as bland a cheese as I had ever tasted. I only hoped that the higher echelons of the French military establishment present did not even begin to suspect my lack of commitment to this particular embodiment of France. I remembered the cheese-tasting ritual at Trebentaz and the fondue-eating ceremony at Moede. Crossing the snow-covered passes of the High Alps of France is relatively safe. Failing to pay due respect to a local cheese *en route* is asking for trouble.

Chapter Twenty-One

An Opportunity Wasted

From Fouillouse, the day's walk is one of two halves; a contrast between the alpine wet and the Mediterranean dry. In the first half, the middle and upper heights on the northern side of the mountain showed alpine landscape at its best. Large sweeps of luscious green pastures were interspersed with small stands of larch trees, set off by the occasional rock outcrop. This was inspiring natural landscape of a scale and beauty beyond the wildest ambitions of Capability Brown; a landscape that need no folly or Greek temple to focus the prospect. But there never was a paradise without a serpent, and here old military works scar the beauty.

The path climbs the Fouillouse Valley alongside the Italian border. Old fortifications of different ages and in various states of dilapidation mark the route. In some places the scenes reminded me of the Highlands of Scotland with their ruins of the barracks of the Hanoverian soldiers who imposed martial law after the Battle of Culloden. Those bleak remnants evoke a feeling of desolation even today, they are so ill-featured both in conception and completion. Yet there are worse examples here. Halfway up the valley, a false Doric Temple would be a significant improvement on the decaying Maginot Line bunker. At Viraysse, at the very head of the valley, there are the grey ruins of barracks set round a regimental square, and above them, on the ridge, the rotting skeleton of a fort dominates the skyline. At ten thousand feet this is the highest fort in Europe and it is a dismal, remote place. The soldiers probably spent their time scheming and lobbying to get a cushier posting with the Foreign Legion in the Sahara. I wandered around the ruined barracks and was saddened to realise that the Army had simply abandoned them to decay. Mentally I petitioned the French authorities to demolish the buildings and tidy up the site, if not on environmental grounds then in respect for the soldiers who served there. A plaque commemorating those men and their regiments would be appropriate. This was not a place to linger and so I moved on to my own cushy posting; a lunch spot at Col Mallemort. When it dawned on me that it translated into the Pass of the Dead Coach, I decided there are too many unnecessary reminders of mortality in the upper Fouillouse Valley and moved on.

The second half of the day was like a walk on the moon, but with gravity. The terrain over the ridge, on the south-facing side, was dry and stony. In marked contrast to the northern slopes, there was not a tree to be seen except far below in the valley bottom. The slopes were broken rock interrupted by patches of grass, but there was no lushness. There was nothing to provide perspective. Two thousand feet below the ridge the landscape eventually began to improve. There were still no trees, apart from a few stunted junipers, but the meadow flora gradually became vibrant as the descent continued. Finally, there was a great carpet of flowers of every shape and size yet strangely limited in colour. Particularly widespread was the delicate and pretty white St Bernard lily thriving in million-fold abundance. It is not dissimilar, at first sight, to our Star of Bethlehem, which grows (reluctantly) in my garden. As a contrast, the orange hawkweed provided small bursts

166

of orange fire amidst the white lilies. People at home dig up hawkweed as an unwanted hairy dandelion. I grow it from seed and encourage it all over my garden for the strength of its blood-orange colour, and because this bloody-minded, odd man out likes the flower.

Even in June there were still plenty of daffodils flowering. Here the variety was the poet's narcissus. Quite how it got its name I do not know. It may refer to the purity of the white petals, more likely it is a reference to the vitriolic, red centre. After the hawkweed patch, every flower was white. White anemones flourished on stalks two feet high and even the buttercups were white. There were acres upon acres of white flowers, as if it had snowed overnight. If the purpose of a flower's colour is to ensure success in attracting pollinating insects, to be one in a billion white flowers is pretty dumb. In the midst of so much white, one single poppy would have had a field day with all the bees.

The village of Larche appeared drab and unappealing from a distance. Rusty tin roofs covered grey, rendered walls with characterless window-openings. Close to, Larche really was drab and unappealing. Apparently the Nazis destroyed the entire village and the French completely rebuilt it in the fifties. What an opportunity wasted, there is not the slightest hint of architectural imagination or even the vaguest suggestion of the warmth of the human spirit in any of the buildings. If I were a student of architecture seeking inspiration but was limited to a choice between Cumbernauld New Town and Larche, I would go to Cumbernauld.

The only exception to the mediocrity was the church, built in 1960 to replace a medieval church dynamited by the Nazis. Uncompromisingly modern, a blue-louvered capping decorated a square white bell-tower to make a building that would look at home in a modern suburb of Stockholm. I could not understand what it was doing here. For me, such deliberate rejection of the local building materials and wilful negligence of the traditions of building that have evolved over hundreds of years in these valleys was, at the very least, incongruous.

I had little choice but to stay at Larche; it was 1.30 p.m. when I arrived and the next place to sleep on the GR5 was eight hours away. I walked straight past the hotel; memorable only for its ugliness. The whole building was dying; unloved and uncared for. I walked straight past the Gîte d'Etape because it looked like a fire station on a trading estate. Everything about it was ultra-modern; it was made of tin and plastic with no windows on three sides. The Auberge looked an entirely better proposition. Standing slightly aloof from the village, as well it might, it was a cheerful, yellow-rendered building with neat, stained window shutters and a large terrace on the south side. There were even some flower boxes – a startling innovation for Larche. Its brightness had attracted all the visitors, like yellow flowers attracting the bees, and there was no accommodation left for me. I had no choice but to retrace my steps and book into the fire station.

On the upside, the fire station had a charming duty manageress; quiet, unassuming but full of confidence. On the downside, I would have to share the premises with forty school-children. These were not the cool, mature eighteen-year olds who had entertained me at Ceillac, these were twelve-year olds and large groups of twelve-year olds simply do not come quietly. I just had to hope that they went to bed early. I need not have worried. They had been on a nature walk that afternoon and returned exhausted. Some fell asleep as their teacher tried to give them an outdoor botany lesson on the flowers they had collected. They ate their supper and tumbled off to bed. Conveniently, I slept on the ground floor and they slept on the second floor and I heard not a sound from them all night.

Now I had to sort out my problem with maps; my Topo Guide ran out here so I had no route-finder or accommodation-guide for the onward trek. Although the footpath signage was generally good, it would be foolhardy to go into the mountains without a map. The Auberge manager advised me that I would have to go twenty miles to Barcelonette, the nearest town, where there would be a wide range of maps and guides. No doubt the town also would have the luxury of a Gents' Outfitter. I had no choice but to hitch-hike, even though returning might be difficult. I stood at the edge of the village, raised my thumb and the very first car screeched to a stop. The gods were smiling on me, for the driver turned out to be the agreeable duty manageress. *'Ah Madame. Allez-vous a Barcelonette?'*

'Oui, Monsieur.'

I jumped into the car and we were off.

'Monsieur, pourquoi allez-vous a Barcelonette?'

'Ah, Madame. C'est très important pour moi, parce que j'ai besoin d'une carte.'

She stamped on the brakes, screeching to a tyre-burning halt. What had I done? How had I offended her? She turned round and drove me back to the village.

'Monsieur,' she said, smiling sweetly. *'Voila l'Office de Turisme de Larche.* It is open at three o'clock and sells maps.' She did not say 'You daft Englishman' but I suspect she thought it.

I used the time saved to acquaint myself with the history of Larche. This, an old frontier town on the Grand Route between Piedmont and Provence, has witnessed the perpetual movement of beasts, merchandise and men across the border. In the Middle Ages, sixty thousand French sheep wintered in Italy, and hundreds of young Italians summered in France helping with the harvest. For a long period local people thought nothing of boundaries and on both sides of the Col de Larche they spoke the same Provençal Alpin dialect. Local people need peace to farm and to trade. Unfortunately, politicians need to make laws and divide people to satisfy their self-importance and kings, of course, need to win glory to justify their existence. The young Francis I of France swept over the border in 1515and defeated the Italian army. Covered in fame and glory, the king returned to Paris with strengthened reputation. Good for him. To the local people, the victory meant an increase in taxes for the politicians to spend on defences to deter the Italian king from coming to get his own back. The politicians undermined the general good neighbourliness of the area by insisting on a defined border between the Bourbons and the Hapsburgs. Far away in Utrecht, in 1713, they drew a line through the Col de Larche and informed the people on each side that they were different. Sensibly, the local people took little notice; pilgrims moved freely in both directions without hindrance and, right up until the last World War, young Italians continued to spend their summers as agricultural labourers on the French side. Such impact of big politicians on small people makes you realise that we would all benefit from fewer politicians, fewer regulations and far less government.

Dinner was another sociable occasion with all the adults crammed together on the balcony while the children created pandemonium in the dining room. We delayed the start of the meal to await the arrival of Irene and Walter, who had taken a wrong turn high up in the mountains. There was nothing remarkable about this German couple at first sight, both of fairly nondescript, flaxen-haired, Saxon stock. But when Irene spoke she switched on like a light bulb; she radiated beauty, her eyes met yours with directness and sparkle, her smile transfused every part of her face as she attended to everything you said with the greatest interest. We were fourteen, French, English and German, eating together at that, communal table and she kept all fourteen in the conversation, deftly translating from French to English to French whenever the situation demanded. Walter's job was easy; he had only to smile in support.

I was walking this trip happily out of step with everyone else. The rest of the world sat hunched watching the World Cup on television screens in darkened rooms. I was enjoying the exhilaration and challenge of the open air. I had decided months back that this would be a good time to be on the GR5. In the first place the route and accommodation would be less crowded than usual. In the second place, the endlessly trivial football reportage would pass me by. No pub arguments for me about referees' mistakes and footballers' cheating. I was in a league of my own and would walk alone in the wilderness. Mind you, I would be home in time for the knockout stages.

Slightly disdainful I might be, but I still wanted to keep track of England's progress. After all, I had been at Wembley for that memorable final in 1966 and ever since, I have lived in the hope of a repetition of the result, if not the drama, of that day. By the time of the England-Sweden match I was in Larche. The only public television set was in the bar of the Auberge so I strolled in just after nine to watch the match. For some reason, beyond my French comprehension, the set could receive a recording of that afternoon's game but not a live broadcast of the evening game. The match between such hot contenders as Paraguay and Trinidad was less than exciting, but I hoped to pick up some reference to the score in the live England game. When I heard that England had scored, I relaxed and went to bed. In the morning, nobody in Larche seemed aware that England had played the night before, let alone the final result. I texted my wife, expecting she would tell me the score soon enough.

Chapter Twenty-Two

Russian Bears Hunt Italian Wolves

The walk out of Larche on a sunny June morning was idyllic. The path set out amongst woodland in the upper reaches of the Ubayette Valley, then, when very nearly over the border into Italy, it swung south into the beautiful Lauzanier Valley, climbing imperceptibly into open grassland, thinly interspersed with larch and pine. I had walked for an hour when I caught up with Khrushchev and his Minder. Khrushchev, of course, was that bear of a Russian leader with a round bald head, sticking-out ears and bulging eyeballs; his great bull neck swelled belligerently as if always he was looking for a fight (he famously once pounded the table with his shoe in the middle of Harold Macmillan's speech to the United Nations General Assembly. Macmillan urbanely replied, "I should like a translation of that remark." I seem to remember the Assembly dissolving into laughter and I felt the first thaw in the Cold War). Here was his double, walking the GR5 with a heavy pack, his greeting more of a grunt than a smile. His Minder, also heavily loaded, was the archetypal prison warder with grey, short-cropped hair, a two-day stubble and a grizzly, weathered face. His greeting was a similar grunt. I quickened my pace and walked on alone.

Part of the famous National Parc of Mercantour, the Lauzanier Valley is a world-famous magnet for professional botanists and all flower lovers. There is a small lake creating a focal point at the head of the valley; turquoise blue in the sunshine and surrounded by billowing waves of flowers in all directions. Predominantly yellow and orange with the blue lake at its centre, the whole head of the valley must look like one gigantic flower from outer space. Further up the hillside the Queen of the Alps displayed her blue-crowned heads by the thousand. This was the Eryngium alpine, a lively, light-coloured close cousin of the darker more sedate Sea Holly which grows in my garden.

Naturally, the longer that I was ignorant of the result of that football match the more I wanted to know. Once I had gained a reasonable height, I texted Jo again asking for the score but there was no reception then or for the rest of the day. I extended minimal courtesies to everyone that I met on the route before interrogating them.

'What football match?' was the standard reply.

Occasionally, somebody expressed a vague interest in football, but admitted they had no knowledge of any Group other than the one which included France. On my way up I met six Americans coming down. Fit, outgoing worldly types, they had no idea what a Football World Cup was, let alone that one was currently under way. Surely soon, almost twenty-four hours after the event, I would meet somebody who knew the result.

The Americans compensated for lack of interest in football by an unbelievable passion for walking-poles. They took their walking seriously and they were most concerned for my safety ('He is in *sandals*, without a stick and all!'), telling me that not far ahead, the path crossed two, deep snowfields on steep slopes. All six of them strongly urged that I should go back down a couple of thousand feet and cut myself a pair of stout tree-branches to use as walking-poles; several of them thought I should go back to England for my boots and ice-axe! Probably at least one of them wanted to excommunicate me for my heretical practises. Of course, I ignored them. Did I not have the experience of the snowfields on Mont Thabor and Col de Ayes behind me? I went up to survey the problem. There was nothing to worry about; the six Americans in their passing had stamped out horizontal ledges across the drifts so crossing them presented no difficulty. Going south I was to come across no more snow. Metaphorically, I could now safely throw away the ice-axe that I really should have brought with me.

The ridge here formed another significant watershed on my walk. The great mass of the high French Alps lay behind me; in front lay the less majestic Alpes Maritime. Until now, all the rivers and streams I had walked along and crossed ultimately drained into the basin of the Rhône, which reached the Mediterranean through the Camargue Delta. From here on, the rivers would be entirely Provençal, all feeding into the River Var and untimately into the Mediterranean at Nice. I could finish the rest of my journey on a raft if I chose.

The descent from Pas de Pavale was the most hair-raising section of the whole GR5 from Lake Geneva to the Mediterranean. The route descended diagonally across the face of a vertical cliff over one hundred feet high and then tracked across steep and treacherous screes. It was a remarkable narrow path, seldom more than two feet wide, cut from the cliff with pick-axes, strain and sweat. At points the path had collapsed and I had to hop a couple of feet from ledge to ledge. Little slips on small jumps can have big consequences when there was a drop of a thousand feet to the rocky scrap heap below. The descent demanded concentration and self-control, which it got from me in unstinted measure. The going was no less dangerous in the scree.

Slowly the palette of colours in the middle distance drew my attention from the dangers immediately in front of me. At first, the landscape was blue, bright electronic blue, with acres upon acres of forget-me-nots. These eventually gave way to rolling masses of yellow *fer-a-cheval*, a plant not dissimilar to our yellow vetch. Finally, the colours spilled across the canvas with flowers of stroboscopic pink, deep orange, light blue, deep blue and whites of all shapes and sizes. The huge variety of flowers produced a matching abundance of butterflies. Particularly eye-catching here was a small orange butterfly, the male Scarce Copper, nondescript and scarcely noticeable with its wings closed but a brilliant spark of explosive orange when flying.

The flower meadows stopped abruptly at the desert of the Salse Morene Valley. Why this huge, desolate expense of stone, with its great ravines gauged out by snow-melt, revelled in the title of Brown Sauce Valley was hard to grasp. It was a battleground of a lunar landscape, the scene of eternal violence between the enduring passive strength of stone against the intermittent, furious, active power of surging water. Since water is indestructible there will only be one victor of the battle, the only question being, How many million years?

Running a National Park is a very serious business. At every point of access numerous boards are needed, telling the visitor what to do. Generally, there are short lists of what he can do and very long lists of what he cannot do. They reminded me of 1950s seaside boarding houses – 'Guests must not return before 7 o'clock'. On the Col des Fourche it was even worse. There were the ubiquitous 'Do Not' notice boards, but here they were guarded on both sides by huge World War Two concrete gun emplacements, with the gun slits lined up to hold the innocent reader in enfilade. There were no machine-guns poking out, but it was a foreboding sight all the same. Nobody drops litter on the Col des Fourche.

On the path was a small bird's egg, perhaps half an inch in length and pale turquoise blue in colour. Fabergé could not have improve its beautiful simplicity. It was stone-cold and abandoned. How infinitely sad that such an exquisite object would not, after all, give life to a beautiful bird, but would merely be guzzled by some ugly little scavenger.

A light drizzle accompanied me all the way down from the heights to the ancient hill village of Bousieyas. It was raining, it was 4 p.m., and the next stop was three hours away. The decision on where to stop was not going to be difficult. One look at the village and I realised that it was in a time-warp so, of course, I decided to stay there. There were four farmhouses, large stone-built structures with timber-shingle roofs. Nothing had changed to the buildings of the village in the last century. In those hundred years, the economic framework of the village had collapsed bringing the social structure down with it. It would have been a slow creeping death as the younger generation left for pastures new and the older generation stayed on in the ever-fading hope that their children would return. Perhaps I imagined the tired despair in the atmosphere. Today the Park Authorities are struggling to restore the buildings to their proper cheerfulness by finding alternative economic uses for them. They have got off to a good start. One roof has recently been re-tiled in wooden shingles; an uplifting sight amongst the depression.

One of the buildings was now a Refuge but when I enquired of Mademoiselle if she had a bed for me she did not know: the Patron had driven off taking the booking chart with him.

'When will he be back?'

'I don't know, perhaps in ten minutes, perhaps in two hours!'

'Can I have a beer while I wait?'

'I am sorry; I do not have the key to the cabinet'.

'Do you know who won the football match last night?'

'*Quoi?*'

Obviously the football results would still have to wait.

'Can I have a shower in the meantime?'

'*D'accord*, Monsieur, come this way'.

I decided to have a shower, get some laundry done and wait for the Monsieur. If the worst came to the worst, I would hitch-hike down the road until I found a bed. In the event, by the time I had washed both myself and my clothes, Mademoiselle had been in touch with Monsieur and found that there was a bed available for me in the Upper House. Regrettably, that did not imply a sudden uplift in my social status, simply that there was a stiff outside climb to the dormitory block up the hill. The Upper House turned out to be a farmhouse that had lain derelict for decades. Monsieur had converted it into sleeping accommodation with absolutely no expense incurred if he could avoid it. Steep and twisting staircases without banisters, surface wiring with dangling switches and hanging points, the Upper House was the ultimate example of penurious DIY and visible proof that in France building inspectors are a rare, if not an endangered, species above four thousand feet. Still the bed was large enough and it had the crowning advantage of being where I was and not three hours further down the road.

I had been settled in for a few hours, done my laundry, wandered around the village and was about to sit down for dinner when in trudged Khruschev with his Minder. Not for the first time on this trip, I learned the salutary lesson of the stupidity of making judgements on first impressions. Across the dinner table the men, that I had summarily dismissed as boorish Russian bears on the route, had infectious smiles, warm eyes, much humour and considerate table manners. Perhaps Khrushchev had spent those intervening years at a Finishing School. Despite their looks, they were French not Russian and over several trips they had been walking the GR5 from the French Luxembourg border. Like The Scottish Saints they carried camping equipment. They had carried it for forty days and used it twice. Self-flagellation would be easier. I multiplied the ten thousand grammes extra weight of their camping equipment by the three hundred and fifty thousand metres that they had walked in a hopeless attempt to calculate the trillions of ergs of unnecessary work that they had done. Just for two night camping. That was not for me. Why buy an insurance policy with the premium guaranteed to be more than the claim? On the other hand, I had only started my walk on the Swiss border and they had walked twice as far as me to get this point. In GR5 seniority terms they were long-service medallists.

The Upper House had a collection of old farmhouse kitchen objects. They all related to a way of life in large farmhouse kitchens at least a century ago and so were entirely outside my experience. Khrushchev was as inquisitive as I was and he proved to be much smarter in working out the purpose of most of the implements. That is understandable; the Russian leader, I remember, had had a peasant background and was always quoting the earthy maxims of his grandmother. My own grandmother did service below stairs in London and her maxims were earthy enough. There was a large, oblong chest made of larch wood, which Khrushchev decided was used to mix dough; enough dough for the farmer's family, and probably all his labour force, for a month. I was not convinced. Why should anyone mix more dough than they needed for the next baking session? I thought that the coffin-size chest must have a more sinister explanation but I let my thoughts rest in peace. Beside the chest was a long-poled, wooden, spade, similar to the implement that the modern-day Italians use for cooking pizzas. Periodically, according to Khrushchev, the farmer's wife would arm herself with the spade and a bucketful of dough from the chest and march off for a big baking and gossip session at the large, communal village oven. The bread baked would be none the worse for the spice of scandal.

Khrushchev and his Minder had been looking for wolves during their trek through these particular mountains. Alpine heights are a natural habitat for wolves and they were only eradicated in the French Alps by disproportionate, if not, all-out warfare in the nineteenth century. They were shot, poisoned with arsenic or caught in pits covered with branches and baited with meat. The last, indigenous wolf died near Ceillac in the 1850s. Apparently, wolves are now mustering the courage to return and are crossing into the French Alps from Italy in increasing numbers.

The European Union, in yet another demonstration of its infinite wisdom and of its sensitivity to the pulse of the population, has decreed the wolf to be a protected species. The local farmers see them as a menace – not unreasonable, since wolves are large, carnivorous animals with sharp claws, drooling fangs and a hearty appetite for lamb. A farmer on an alpine ridge, shotgun in hand with his lambing flock below and a wolf in his sights above, may be thankful that Brussels and its bureaucrats are a long way away. Perhaps that is why neither Khrushchev nor I have yet seen a wolf.

Chapter Twenty-Three

The Kissing Postmistress

There is a pincer movement at work in the French Alps. From the north the ski-ing industry is creeping southwards like a glacier, taking over villages and replacing their originality and character with tin boxes. From the south the holiday-home market is crawling northwards colonising villages, tidying them up and preserving them so that they became a manicured caricature of their original selves. Sooner or later these two pincers will meet and by then, the soul will have been bitten out of the French Alps.

After Bousieyas, St Dalmas-le-Selvage was an enjoyable example of an alpine village still more or less doing its own thing and as yet escaping the pincers. It was attractive, neither disfigured nor prettified and it got the thumbs-up from me for having a majority of wood shingle roofs. The local grey building stone was un-dressed and un-coursed and blended well with the understated greys and creams of the wall renders. Flowerboxes were full of colour in a profusion not seen since Ceillac. The ultimate proof that the village was in its own happy time capsule was its lack of mobile phone coverage. I was usually happy about this, but not to-day; I wanted to know the football score. It was thirty-eight hours since the final whistle; would I ever find out if we had won or lost?

The mixed woodland below St Dalmas was home to a wide variety of insect life. Given my clothing, I tended to be wary of the buzzy, biting types, but I was attracted to a most improbable creature which was neither one thing nor another. It reminded me of a gangly schoolboy that does not know what he wants to be when he grows up. This insect had reached an evolutionary stage where it looked half butterfly and half dragonfly. It had the short body and broad wings of a butterfly but with the wing-transparency typical of a dragonfly. At the crossroads of evolution, who knew where evolutionary pressures would take this strange creature next? When I eventually got to an English reference book I found that it rejoiced under the popular name of the Broad-bodied Libellula, or was it the Broad-bellied Libodula? Either way, the scientists classify it as a Darter Dragonfly, but I prefer my theory that it is a missing link.

The route wound back down into the Valley at St Etienne de Tinée, an outpost of the old fiefdom of the Counts of Nice. It was an interesting place with narrow streets of four or five storey, terraced buildings, each painted in attractive pastel renders. The town square was small and colourful with a yellow-rendered church and a pink-painted Marie competing for the souls and minds of the townsfolk. Faith and Reason glared at each other flamboyantly and competitively with just a small grey area of tarmac between them. Ths grey area was highly symbolic, but it was hardly big enough to accommodate all us 'don't knows' in between.

Ever since I had struggled up to Henri's Refuge from Modane ten days ago, I had been rebelling against the weight of my pack. On every climb I had made mental lists of items I could post back to England. The list grew every day but where was a post office when I needed one? Very few of the settlements *en route* were big

181

enough to justify a post office and those that were, invariably had opening times to suit the Postmistress rather than the Randonneur. I was keen to lighten my pack but not keen enough to lose two hours walk waiting for the office to open at 10 a.m. After days of near-misses, I found myself in St Etienne de Tinée before the post office closed for the day. Sending a parcel is so easy in France; there is no need to worry about brown paper, string or sellotape because the Bureau de Poste offers a helpful packaging facility. I presented my goods for dispatch in a plastic bag, the Postmistress gauged the size and gave me a stout, flat-pack cardboard carton. In went the binoculars (too heavy to carry up mountains and anyway I had positively identified the Nutcracker), in went several maps and the Topo Guide of the route behind me. Exposed films, completed notebooks, local guidebooks were all packed. I dithered over the French butterfly identification book I had bought in Briançon. It was heavy and included large sections on obscure genera only of interest to the most dedicated entomologist; on the other hand the quarter of the book devoted to butterflies and moths contained superb, detailed drawings. To walk the route without attempting to identify the great variety of butterflies found on the GR5 would be like walking with my eyes closed. I remembered my attitude to the Swankee Yankees; the book would stay!

I handed the packed box over to the Postmistress who sealed it and took my money. Impressed by the efficiency of the whole operation, I smiled through the glass partition and, as a form of thank-you, said, '*Vive l'Entente Cordiale.*'

She smiled, stood up, unlocked the office-door, came through and kissed me on the cheek.

'*Vive l'Entente Cordiale,*' she echoed. I think I will post parcels more often.

On the climb up the hill to Auron, lavender grew beside the path. I sat on a rock, picked handfuls of leaves and flowers and rubbed them all over my arms, neck legs and every inch of bare skin that I could find. It worked miracles. Not only did I smell of grandma's clean linen but my phone began to burr-burr with pleasure. Obviously lavender has some therapeutic effect on the air-waves, because text messages started to stream in. At last, I learned the result of that match: Sweden had held England to a draw. Sometimes ignorance is bliss.

The Topo Guide waxed eloquently about the numerous hotels in Auron. It neglected to mention that only one was open during the summer and that, as a result, the place was a ghost town. I suppose I cannot have it both ways. I cannot relish the peace and solitude of walking along barely-used footpaths, if I want the resorts to be full of company in the summer.

At least I did manage to find a bar that was open. The flaxen-haired Dutch barmaid helpfully directed me to the one hotel open in the town; the Pine Marten Logi run by Yvette and Pierre. Yvette was a most attentive hostess. No sooner had I sat down in the reception area than she was offering me coffee. Somehow she slipped and poured the hot liquid into my lap instead of into my cup. She was mortified and apologised profusely.

'Do you need treatment for scalding?'

'Can I clean your trousers?'

'Please take your trousers off!'

The only way that I could calm her down (and keep my dignity) was to make light of the incident and pretend that a scalded thigh was nothing and that coffee-stained trousers did not matter – not entirely true, since I had yet to find a Gents' Outfitter.

The hotel was too up-market to have a clothes-line for guests who were expected to be too genteel to display their wet smalls in public. Mine hosts overcame my problem by putting all my washing into their spin-dryer. Chores complete, I settled down to a beer on the terrace only to see Clickety-clack coming into town with exactly the same, distinctive gait that had so endeared him to me when I had first seen him six days ago.

I wandered around Auron determined to root out its best features. I started with the church. The tradition in the Tinée

Valley is for Romanesque churches which have a short, fairly squat, stone tower with lancet openings on each face, surmounted by a stone spire. With little ornament but the inevitable French cockerel on top of the spire, the churches present a stolid, unexciting air from St Dalmas to here at Auron. I wondered how it was that the cockerel, symbol of the secular, French Revolution, come to sit atop the House of God. But, of course, were I a Frenchman I would know that indubitably God is French. The church nave has the distinction of a timber-shingle roof, albeit one rather clumsily built over a corrugated-iron petticoat. This was not a stunning building but it had its points of interest, not least that it had been there for nigh on a thousand years.

I went to bed in a benevolent frame of mind, wishing good will to all men. I drew back the curtains to ensure that I woke early in the morning and took it all back. All through the hours of darkness that fine church has its delicate lancet windows in its ancient Romanesque tower illuminated by lurid, pink neon strip-lights. Pink neon lights in a Norman church tower are a desecration beyond belief. I hate ski-resorts!

184

Chapter Twenty-Four

A Five-Star Cowshed

The Dutch barmaid saw me go by as I was leaving and she came out to ask how I had enjoyed the Hotel.

'It was good,' I said. 'I had only been there an hour and Madame asked me to take my trousers off!'

She thought for a moment then looked at me with her tongue poked into her cheek and a twinkle in her eye.

'That's France for you,' she said. 'In Holland you would have to wait for a couple of hours.'

With a deadpan face, I said, 'Perhaps, but in England you could wait for ever!'

Walkers coming north had warned me of a collapse of the footpath just south of Auron.

'You must walk up the piste,' they advised.

Yvette and Pierre had given me the same advice in the casual tone of voice usually employed to discuss a walk in the park. Pistes are designed for skiers to have fun zooming down; nobody gives a thought to back-packers plodding up. It was steep, so steep that even zigzagging spelt danger for the ankles. I was half way up before I realised that nobody who had so considerately advised me to 'walk up the piste' had actually done so.

As ever, the ridge was worth the climb. I was on top of the world again with larch parkland landscape all around me, surmounted by rocky cliffs, stone towers and ridges in all directions. A dianthus of such intense colour that it appeared to be luminous intrigued me. *Dianthus carthusianorum* is a magenta rather than a pink, so deep is its colour. A single flower, no more than half an inch across was so bright that I could see it at fifty paces. Since there were acres of the flowers around I was glad I was wearing photo-chromatic glasses. The path was hard to follow as it picked its way up through the colour but easily traceable as I descended, striking a sensible angle across the contours. Roya, a neat, attractive and remote settlement suddenly appeared below. When I reached it, I drowned my memories of difficult pistes in the guzzling of mineral water, ice-cold and très gaseous!

The waiter was a cheerful, friendly man and I have every reason to believe that he really wanted to be helpful.

'It is only the next five hours that are difficult,' he said. 'After that it is easy!'

He has to be a better barman than he is a psychologist. I was not particularly pleased to know that the next five hours would be sheer hell, whereas the subsequent three would be only normally painful. Why did he not do the decent thing and lie to me? 'The first hour is hard but after that it is a really enjoyable stroll.'

As it turned out, the walk was an unmitigated delight; as good a day's walk as I can remember. Leaving the Roya valley, the path wound up the course of a tributary. Initially the climbing was steep and uninteresting, but when I reached the tree-line I discovered that the path had led me to the focal point of a huge, awesome landscape. Ahead were two enormous cirques, gigantic amphitheatres of rocks, each about two miles in diameter and both with scree slopes supporting vertical cliffs some hundreds of feet high. I felt like an insignificant dot at the centre of a curved capital E, like a gigantic Euro sign lying on its side.

The path took an easy-going course, slowly gaining height, and heading into the left-hand cirque. Try as I may, I could see no reasonable way out over the cliff wall now facing me. There was bound to be a difficult scramble ahead and perhaps I should do it on a full stomach. I stopped for lunch as the path crossed a stream more or less at the centre-point of the semi-circle of cliffs.

When I had considered today's walk from the comfort of the Pine Marten Logi, the book had advised that there was nine and half hours of walking to Refuge Longon. In case I did not get that far and I had to stay out somewhere overnight, I had asked for two packed lunches. Pierre must have thought I was provisioning a regiment; he had given me a huge amount of food. For one lunch he had provided quarter of a pound of pâté and a similar amount of cheese, a generous loaf, a hard-boiled egg, an orange, two tomatoes and four apricots. I ate the lot, as I sat at the water's edge, dabbling bare feet in cold, running water. I was beset by enormous flies about an inch across and in the shape of Tornado jets. They were black, noisy, sinsister and aggressive. Conscious that this was an off-day, I scurried up the slope looking for a no-fly zone.

The climb up that cliff confirmed all my worst fears. Once again, the route suited an athletic fell-runner skipping down rather than a geriatric walker trudging up. Yet, as with all the seemingly impossible ridges behind me, in the fullness of time I breached the cirque and conquered those high cliffs. I had climbed two severe slopes in one day and it was only 2 p.m. My reward was to find that there was a second, even larger, cirque ahead of me. Fortunately, it was not as overpowering as the first; I could pick out the route ahead following a reasonable gradient. The walls, formed by steep rock boulder slopes, embraced on three sides a beautiful, green hanging valley. At last, eight hours after starting up the piste at Auron, and five hours after watering at Roya, I reached the ridge. When I looked back down into the valley from the final cliff-top some forty minutes later, I saw a small herd of grazing chamois. They must have hidden themselves in a secret hollow as I walked past and watched me with those sad, limpid eyes. The hard bit was behind me. Now, according to the waiter, it would be easy.

Normally, almost by definition, the path goes downhill after a col, but the topography was topsy-turvy at Col de Crousette. The path climbed diagonally upwards at a gradient of about 1 in 4 across a rugged scree slope that plunged down dramatically at a gradient of about 1 in 2. Now that *is* steep. On that slope I felt like a tiny ant lost in a gigantic Escher drawing. The contrasting angles were disorientating and I felt distinctly uncomfortable, if not slightly scared. The odds of a slip were reasonably low, but the consequences would be serious; a fall down a thousand feet rock slope in an area where I had not seen another walker all day. I selected my footing very slowly and carefully, concentrating on my balance and making no attempt at any geometric analysis. I should have shot that waiter.

By the time I had overcome the danger I was standing on a flanking ridge of the great Mont Mounier with the summit not far above me. It was 4 p.m. The Topo Guide was quite clear; it was a three-hour walk to Refuge Longon. A signpost indicated that the walk would take four-and-a-half hours. Ever the optimist, I ignored the local information, and I rang ahead to book a bed and a meal at the Refuge telling them with cheerful confidence that I would be there by 7 p.m. How had I forgotten so quickly the lesson I had learned at Montgenevre?

I walked briskly down south-facing slope – an arid, lunar landscape where I half expected Neil Armstrong to appear in his space suit at any moment. The vegetable kingdom began its struggle for the colonisation of this elevated desert with a wizened old crone of a plant that had emaciated and leathery, cabbage-like leaves and a yellow thistle-like flower. Its Latin name is *Berardia subacaulis* but it is such a specialist plant restricted to the higher levels of the Alps that the gardeners have never got round to giving it a common name, let alone attempting to cultivate it.

After a couple of hours walking down from the col, a cluster of roofs appeared ahead. I was pleased, it looked as though the Topo Guide was right and I was about to arrive at my stop for the night. The mirage turned out to be nothing but an abandoned village. If anyone is looking for a business opportunity, then open a Gîte d'Etape at Vignols; a small, mostly deserted village at the very end of the road system at the head of the Tinée Valley. It lies a few hundred yards off the GR5 path; eight hours walk northwards for Roya and six hours southwards for Roure, perfectly located to serve walkers travelling in either direction. An entrepreneurial businessman could widen his customer-base with such modern, life-style service products as a Buddhist Meditation Retreat, an alcohol rehabilitation centre and a Commando survival skill training-centre, although he should not perhaps run all the courses at the same time.

A smart Randonneur would have realised hours ago that the local signs were right and the guidebook was wrong. I had been walking for twelve and a half hours, mostly uphill and with only a few stops. I was tired, but my spirits were high and I was far from exhausted. I walked triumphantly into Refuge Longon at 8.30 p.m. I expected to be hustled into through dinner so that the Refuge owners could clear up for the night. Not a bit of it. Stephan and Lauren were kindness and consideration personified.

'Have a beer. Would you like to eat, or shower first?'

I showered in cold water. I did not care much. I was obviously far tougher than the wimp who had splashed about at Lac Sainte Marguerite.

Once I was clean and refreshed I realised just how hungry I was. Stephan served me a meal that Lauren had cooked, not the leftovers from the communal fare that they had provided hours earlier, but as if I was an honoured guest and everything had been prepared especially for me. I ladled out several bowls from a large cauldron of steaming hot vegetable soup. They served the main course, rich, hot ravioli à la Provençal, in an individual oven dish just for me. The cheese came from the Haute Languedoc; Roquefort, which, to me, is the Emperor of French cheeses. Finally the dessert, *poivres aux épices et au vin*, was as good as you would find in the best restaurants from Paris to Marseilles. I could hardly believe that I was being fed like a king in a simple shed way up in the mountains where supplies came in by helicopter and where energy was too expensive to provide a hot shower.

The youngest hosts that I met on my trip, Stephan and Lauren were possibly the highest-qualified. There were newspaper cuttings on the wall featuring Lauren excelling on catering courses and Stephan studying forestry. Here was a light-hearted yet serious-minded pair who enjoyed running a remote Refuge and who applied themselves diligently to all matters of hospitality and of the environment. While Lauren was setting the table for breakfast, Stephen was pulling heavy botany books off the shelves helping me to identify my wizened old crone of a cabbage long after the sun had set behind Mont Mounier.

A cowshed at Longon is a far cry from the Savoy, but after those many hours of walking in the mountains, its cold shower, delicious meal, congenial hosts and bunk bed were five-star luxury to me.

Chapter Twenty-Five

Sour Grapes for Dinner

I spent a few minutes exploring the old buildings of the Refuge. Why should anyone choose to build here in such a remote spot four hours by packhorse from anywhere? The answer was cheese. The Refuge was a *vacherie*, restored after being hit by an avalanche in 1936. I found it hard to accept that within living memory, people had earned their living keeping cows and making cheese so high up in this distant hanging valley. It must have been a hard and lonely life.

Starting a day with a four-hour downhill walk is a rare treat on the GR5. The path picks its way across open larch parkland before dropping down into denser, deciduous woodland. Now that I was well into the Southern Alps, the woods were lush with the green foliage of massive oaks interspersed with delicate field maple, wild cherry, Spanish chestnut and even the occasional fig tree.

I had walked down the track for an hour when I stopped and rubbed my eyes in disbelief. A young family was tending a herd of about thirty of the now-familiar Tarentais cows. They were setting up a new *vacherie*. If cheese-making became uneconomical in the

191

thirties, how could it be viable today? Even with a niche market, this was surely hopelessly, romantically impractical. That may be, but they do have one distinct advantage over their 1936 predecessors. Today they access the outside world by means of a stonking great four-by-four. Remembering my previous unhappy encounter with four-wheel drive vehicles at Bionnassay, I decided that this particular monster was acceptable if it got children to school and cheese to market.

I had not gone much further when I noticed a group of cows huddled on the hillside above me. They were perhaps half a mile away and not easy to pick out individually. I could see a man standing off from the group. I tried to work out what was happening. Why the stand-off? If the man had gone to bring them in for milking, why did he not get on with it? Then I realised that one of the cows was lying down, being licked by the other cows. I sat on a tree-trunk trying to work out what was going on in that strange tableau. The prostrate cow stood up, wobbled and collapsed, surrounded by her attentive sisters. The man began to drag something down the hill and it all clicked into place in my slow, townsman's mind. The cow had just given birth and was weak. The calf had either been born dead or had died soon after birth. Knowing the herd would be dangerous and unpredictable in that situation, all he could do was to keep his distance until he could haul away the dead calf.

While the man came down the hill, the cows slowly returned to grazing, leaving the sick mother to recover by herself. Down came a heron to breakfast on the afterbirth. The incident was over. I hoisted on my pack in sombre mood; I did not want to meet the farmer dragging the dead calf. It was a tough world out there, brutal and uncompromising; poor cow – there is no trauma-counselling for bovines.

Roure is the beginning of civilisation if you are a cheese-maker from Longon. To me, it was a small village built on a precipitous cliff-face at the very end of civilisation. The village streets were narrow, stepped alleys with one house stacked on top of another and no room for gardens. It had all the town planning atributes of a kittiwake colony, but wihout the guano. A jumble of rubble and red clay pantiles with only the occasional rusting corrugated iron sheet for contrast; small, thin houses struggled up to four storeys high in a desperate attempt to reach light, like flowers craning for the sun. A law firm would be kept busy in Roure sorting out disputes over property rights, rights of communal uses, ancient lights, rights of access, and so on. Historically, the only reason people would eke out an existence in such conditions, instead of spreading out in the lush valley two thousand feet below, must have been security. When the locals built Roure they were seeking a safe haven in a remotes and lawless world.

I found it hard to visualise just how ordinary people survived in these areas during the hundreds of years between the departure of the Romans and the establishment of law and order under a King's writ. As a matter of fact, the King's writ never did run in the Vesubie Valley. By the time that the area eventually did have the protection of a state's legal and police systems that state had beheaded its King and installed a President.

This valley was part of the ancient territory of the Counts of Nice, the Grimaldis. Historically, they have controlled large parts of the area of the Alpes-Maritime, far larger than their vestigial Principality of Monaco. The family are famous and well-loved international celebrities now, particularly since the marriage of the suave Prince Rainier to the American Movie Goddess, Grace Kelly. They have sometimes been little varmints in the past. Count Beuil Grimaldi burnt the village and the church at St Etienne de Tinée in 1594 to show his absolute feudal power over both faith and reason.

Beyond the village, the path descended further into the Tinée valley through mixed woodland, mostly oak but with increasing numbers of fig and sweet chestnut. The day before, when the going became hard, I had urged myself on by fantasising over a small hotel with a garden terrace beside a river, cool with running water, colourful with flowers and sunshades, cheerful with smiling hosts. St Sauveur on the River Tinée was billed as the most important town in the valley and I swaggered in around high noon expecting fulfilment of my fantasies. I had walked through the place in five minutes. There was no flower-bedecked, garden terrace. Worse still, there was no Gents' Outfitter. Neither was there a chemist, which left me with a problem since I had run out of water purification tablets. I decided to walk on and to keep a tighter grip on my fantasies in future. The last building of the town redeemed the whole situation. It was a bar serving food, admittedly beside a road rather than a river, but it did serve a handsome melon and ham salad. I had just ordered when a cohort of a dozen, black-leathered, Swiss bikers brrm-brrrmed in and sat at an adjacent table. They were umming and aahing over the various menu choices when my eight-Euro medley was served. Four luscious quarters of a juicy melon, draped generously with sheets of ham, laid on a bed of mixed salad, all set off by a spring onion rising vertically from the centre, its stalk fanned out to form a parasol. It was a beautiful, voluptuous, X-certificate of a salad. The Swiss stopped debating and ordered twelve of the same.

Revitalised by the lunch, I wandered back through the village in a more positive frame of mind. The delights of the place were subtle but all the more pleasing and worth the finding for that. The predominant architectural style was shabby-genteel with an abundance of discreet and interesting detail. The houses were a jumble of delicate cast-iron balconies, Provençal-coloured renders faded to pastel shades, old stone door jambs and lintels. Some of the lintels had faint evidence of old carvings describing the trade of the original occupant, like a comb for a hairdresser or perhaps a wigmaker, and a sheep for a wool merchant. The Government had designed the most interesting building – and there are not many towns where that is true. The Ministry of Agriculture apparently begat a Department of Water and Forests which in its turn begat a Fisheries Section. It is hard to believe that such bureaucratic forbears could give birth to a thing of beauty, yet it is so. The Fisheries Section Depot in St Sauveur was a long warehouse of stone with the windows framed in red brick. Elegantly proportioned, it had a glass canopy running above the ground floor windows for the whole front elevation. A painted panel almost a metre high, depicting fish in river settings, covered the length of the building between the first-floor windows and the eaves. Finally, a central gabled peak carried further decoration including the name of the Department, all strongly framed in a painted timber. It was as though a French Charles Rennie Macintosh, exiled to a remote outpost, had taken his revenge by using the construction budget as an art fund.

Body and soul nourished, I decided to tackle the two thousand feet climb to Rimplas. A couple of miles along the track and who should I find there to greet me but my faithful guardian, St Roch? I had missed him on the middle section of the GR5 where most of the wayside shrines were to the Virgin Mary. Here he was again, a large chapel in a small clearing in the thickly wooded hillside, and he would be with me for the rest of the walk. Like the shrine at Neuteu, it was surprising to find such a well-maintained building in such an isolated position. During my travels, I had learned more about this Pilgrims' Saint. While on a pilgrimage himself, St Roch had come to a village afflicted with the plague. He stayed to minister to the sick, effecting several miraculous cures. Eventually succumbing to the disease himself, he walked off into the forest to die. A dog befriended him, stole food for him and nursed him to recovery. It is easy to see why he is the Patron Saint of Pilgrims. What is less obvious to me is why he is also the Patron Saint of Dogs. Since it was the dog that saved the man, surely the dog deserves the greater credit?

The heat made the climb difficult and I was parched, dusty and sweating by the finish. Surely no mirage this time, there welcoming me to the village of Rimplas was a smart Logi hotel with a terrace, bright with flowers and parasols, overlooking the valley far below. A young barmaid greeted me with a sweet smile. All that I had fantasised about – what a wonderful place to stay. I would enjoy a beer or two on the terrace while I deliberated over the menu and the wine list. As I should have learned this morning, my fantasies never come true. The place was full. The next accommodation was five kilometres further around the mountain at La Bolline.

The disappointment must have shown in my body language because it was then that the first miracle happened. A man stepped forward and volunteered to drive me. I thought, at first glance, that he might be French with his huge drooping moustache, long hair under a straw-boater and a loosely-knotted leather tie. I knew beyond doubt that he was French when he drove his small Citroën round that precipitous, mountain road with one hand on the wheel and the other elegantly emphasising his conversational points. I entered whole-heartedly into the conversation simply to take my mind off the suicidal danger of driving at high speed on the wrong side of a road that was no more than a small shelf cut out of a vertical mountainside. Four times in four kilometres the laws of probability should have ensured that we knocked the other car off the road before we followed it into oblivion. Calmly driving this wall of death, Claude proudly told me that he was a singer and that he was doing a gig at the Rimplas Logi that very evening. He was no ordinary singer, of course, he sang traditional French songs, accompanying himself on the guitar and often wrote his own material. Imagine my anguish. At Rimplas there was a flowered terrace with a view over the river, a Logi demi-pension dinner, a live, traditional French singer; all the ingredients I could ever hope for in a French Shangri-la and yet I was moving on! Claude dropped me off, refusing any contribution to his petrol costs and disappeared round the corner on two wheels, presumably to save wear on the other two tyres.

La Bolline looked to be large enough for one or two decent hotels, so I dropped into a bar for a beer and information. I was told there were no hotels, but there was a Chambre d'Hote just along the road. Happily, it was a charming, double-fronted house that was French in every detail. Sadly, there was no one in. I went back to the bar for a beer. Madame said she would phone the owner. As I drank my beer, I saw a lady enter the house, closely followed by a young man with a small suitcase. I got there to discover that the young man had taken the last room. The lady phoned around for accommodation for me but she could find nothing. I went back to the bar for a beer. Madame of the bar held a conference with Madame of the Chambre d'Hote, then told me that the nearest accommodation was another five kilometres round the mountain and no, there were no taxis. This day was rapidly turning from one of interest to one of exasperation. Then the second miracle happened. The young man with the small suitcase had discovered that he had unknowingly gazumped me over the last room. He insisted that he would drive me to the next village. I discovered that he was a mountain runner and that tomorrow there was an important race. He was going to run ten miles up and down a mountain in about an hour and a half. On that very same day, I was going to plod some twenty miles up and down a mountain and it would take me all day. I vainly tried to justify myself to myself with the thought that I would be carrying more than a vest with a cardboard number-plate.

At the next village of St Dalmas Valdeblore the runner made enquiries at the Office de Tourisme who telephoned around and, *voilà*, I had a room. When we got there I realised that I was some three kilometres off my route and that I had a long enough walk tomorrow anyway. Too bad! I would worry about tomorrow, tomorrow. Today, in my third village, at last I had a bed and a terrace, although it lacked the flowers and there was no river.

The hotel was busy because it was the week-end and there was that big fell-race taking place, but it was grossly short of staff with only Monsieur Sour Grapes at front of house and presumably only his wife running the kitchen. Sour Grapes was a perfectionist; he had spent years disciplining his facial muscles never to show the slightest trace of a smile. He had graduated with distinction and for his doctorate he had gone on to ensure that his eyes should never show a glint of amusement. He was busy, to be sure, running reception, the bar and the dining-room; but if he had to do it, why did he not make the best of it? I fancied a beer on the terrace. Dismissing any hope of table-service I went to the bar and asked timidly for a beer. Sour Grapes glared at my temerity. He yanked off the top and plonked the bottle on the bar, adding a glass only as an afterthought, then he worked his eyebrows with all the display of overworked martyrdom that he could muster. Sour Grapes was big in overworked martyrdom right through the serving of dinner.

Peter, Janet and daughter Gillian rescued me from what promised to be a boring evening. An English family who lived in the Vesubie valley, they had come up to Valdeblore for the night because Peter was going to run the race tomorrow. That was fortunate for me, for I got the benefit of their lively conversation over dinner in the morgue of a dining-room and also a lift back to my GR5 in the morning. At eight years old, Gillian has spent most of her life in France, speaking English at home and French at school. She is happier speaking French which reinforces the idea that children learn language more readily from their playmates than from being on their mother's knee. She had the innocent and transparent honesty of a child when she wrinkled her nose at my poor French. What does an eight year old know!

Chapter Twenty-Six

A Filmset of a Village

In between the *épicerie* at St Dalmas and the square at Utelle was a sixteen mile ridge-walk through one huge forest. The route did not always follow the ridge, sometimes it was a few hundred feet below, but this gave the benefit of a sensibly graded path that did not have to follow every up and down of the actual crest. There were quite steep climbs at either end but for most of the day I enjoyed fairly level walking with fine views in every direction.

Water, normally a major problem on a long ridge walk, was available halfway at Granges de la Brasque. Here were the remains of barrack-like stone buildings and the guidebook made reference to a Military Holiday Camp. Surely that was an oxymoron. I have never yet heard of a soldier who, going on leave, did not get as far away as possible from anything military? The term must surely be a euphemism for something worse, like a Rehabilitation Centre or even a Detention Camp. Even so, there was a certain charm about those stone buildings in their wooded parkland setting and I wondered whether Billy Butlin had ever passed this way as a young man and picked up a few ideas.

John and Anne, a young New Zealand couple from Auckland, were enjoying the fresh water spring at Brasque when I arrived. We shared reminiscences of the Milford Trail on South Island which they claimed to be the most beautiful walk in the world. I agreed that is was so – on the three days a year when it is not raining.

They were walking north along the GR5 but theirs was a semi-organised walk and a carrier transported their luggage for them from one overnight stopping-place to the next. To me this has two distinct disadvantages. In the first place, they must stop each night at a predetermined place. They had surrendered all freedom of choice and were unable to follow any whims of their own. Secondly, they must stop at establishments accessible by road; forgoing the opportunity to enjoy the Refuges away in the high mountains. Those are big issues which I am not prepared to concede; my preference is to cut my pack weight to less than twenty pounds and walk as I choose.

I lazed in the sun, dabbling my feet in the stream. John and Anne hurried on; they could not stop, they had an appointment with a suitcase.

The day included a great deal of woodland walking which became tedious by the time there were no more new trees left to identify. A clearing was welcome because I might catch the rare glimpse of a mammal or might find flowers and insects to appreciate. At one stage, I noticed three of four dark squirrels ahead and expected to see no more of them once they had skittered up the tree. But when I walked under that tree at least three pine cones came down very close to me. Squirrels do not usually dislodge pine cones; the odds on their dislodging three at the same place must be exceptionally long. I think they threw them at me deliberately. Good for them. Why should a big, brute

Homo sapiens blunder through their territory unchallenged. If they perfect their aim, we walkers might have to wear hard hats when walking through the woods.

Le Brec d'Utelle is a rocky pinnacle standing at the end of the ridge which marked the finish of the day's walk, like a lighthouse at the end of the pier. The route, which at this section was another ancient packhorse track, wound round the tower like the chute of an old helter-skelter.

Today England was playing Ecuador in the World Cup and I determined that I would keep up-to-date this time. I texted my son, whom I knew would be in front of a television set somewhere in the world, and I asked him to text me as the game progressed. At kick-off I was on top of Le Brec d'Utelle at 5,300 feet. By the final whistle I had descended 2,600 feet to Utelle. By all accounts, I'd done brill compared to a lack-lustre English squad. I had made the right decision to come walking in the mountains rather than sit at home watching the English squad bumble around with no conviction.

At last, I arrived at Utelle and there to welcome me on the outskirts of the village was a Logi set in a colourful flower garden. What bliss. This was the dream of a Logi in a garden that drove me on. Except that this particular Logi was not a hotel but a set of apartments only rentable by the week and it had no bed for me. The owner gave me a beer and a military-style briefing on the situation. He told me that there was no accommodation in the village except at the Gîte Commune. This is a quite common and most welcome facility in France. It is usually a very basic self-catering hostel which the villagers themselves have provided for the shelter of Randonneurs. According to *mon Colonel*, these particular villagers find it a nuisance and are usually reluctant to open up their facility.

'Be firm!' he commanded, as he very firmly ushered me off his own premises.

'Be firm – insist that they provide you with a bed.'

I was tired and hungry, it was getting late, I could hardly speak the language and I had zero options. 'Being firm' did not appear to me to be my smartest strategy. 'Looking tired and helpless' seemed more likely to succeed under the circumstances. And so it proved in the end! Initially, I made enquiries of Madame in the Corner Bar, who directed me around the corner to Madame in the Village Hall who, in her turn, directed me up the hill to Madame in the White House on the Left. My tired and helpless strategy was getting me shunted from pillar to post. Perhaps I should try the 'be firm' attitude after all. Fortunately, Madame in the White House on the Left proved to be the current Custodian of the Key of the Gîte Commune. She led me back through the village as if showing a prize animal at an agricultural show. Three paces ahead, she swung her hips with some deliberation and acknowledged onlookers as though she was personally responsible for taming this strange, wild-looking creature and bringing it to heel. The Gîte Commune was of a very high standard. As the only occupant, I had the choice of some ten bunks, all with wide and thick mattresses, and the luxury of a high-pressure, hot shower. For this apogee of worldly comforts I paid Madame of the White House on the Left the equivalent of £6 for the night.

It was now 8 p.m., the sun was still out and it was warm, yet the village had shut for the night. I asked Madame of the Corner Bar for the menu. She paused in hoisting chairs onto tables and told me wearily that there was no food because they closed at 8 p.m. She slammed the shutters closed and I sat at an outside table alone with a beer, slowly coming to terms with the fact that I would not have even flavourless spaghetti to mop up my liquid supper. There seemed no alternative to escape the excitement of Utelle on a Sunday evening but to go to bed. Then the shuttered doors opened. Madame appeared with a warm smile. She had taken pity on me and brought out another beer, a large ham salad and a roll. The 'look tired and helpless' strategy

202

may have played its part, but I prefer to think that Madame was just plain nice.

Refreshed, I had no intention of going to bed early; I was going to explore this filmset of a French village. Entrance was gained through a tunnel underneath the church on the one side and a fortified medieval building on the other. This dramatic portal opened into a square only just large enough to give perspective to its enclosing buildings. The Romanesque church formed one side of the central space. It had a large Gothic canopied entrance porch that trespassed into the square, forcing single-lane traffic to manoeuvre carefully and slowly in and out of the tunnel. This ecclesiastical traffic calmer was far more elegant than road humps. It worked harmoniously enough but I shuddered to think what English Engineers would have done – probably flood the place with a plethora of white lines, road signs and even traffic lights on the Gothic columns themselves. The porch protected a pair of exceptional, sculpted doors in the style of the carved doors to the Duomo in Florence, but in wood, rather than bronze. The panels depicted various scenes in the life of St Veran, the Patron Saint of Utelle.

One of the buildings of Utelle is an illusion. Facing the square, it has an attractive, strong façade of mellow-pink, fine-coursed stone, set symmetrically with two levels of fine, full-height windows. Fine stone mullions and a carved stone pediment frame each and its dark-green shutters. What an aristocratic building to find in a humble village; what an elegant contribution to a fine village square. Except that it is a hoax. Only the green shutters, dilapidated on closer inspection, are real, the rest is a *trompe l'oeil* on plain cement render. But so what? It works magic in the little square of Utelle.

The illusion is counter-balanced on the opposite side of the square by the unquestionable solid reality of the stone church. Re-modelled in the sixteenth century, the foundations are probably over a thousand years old. Built on a massive scale, with that Gothic entrance porch big enough to serve a cathedral, the building emanates strength and permanence. Completing the threesome of notable structures in one small village square is a work of art commemorating the history of the last hundred years. A large, white marble fountain, so beautifully made that it would grace any square in any city in Europe, doubles as a War Memorial to the sacrifices made by the families of Utelle in the two World Wars.

Chapter Twenty-Seven

I Sleep with a Countess

Utelle at 8 a.m. bore a striking similarity to Utelle at 8 p.m.; closed and deserted. There was no hope of breakfast, not even a cup of green tea; the luxury of coffee and croissant would have to wait a few hours until I was down the track at Levens.

I did find one lady conscientiously sweeping not only the private entrance to her house, but the whole public area around that entrance. When I congratulated her on the prettiness of the pot plants around her front door her cheeks suffused to match the red of her carnations as she wished me an eternity of happy rambling. The route ahead from Utelle to Levens looked impossible for anything other than a mountain goat. It plunged down the seemingly vertical side of a gorge to the River Vesubie then climbed an equally-high vertical wall on the other side. But, of course, an ancient track, hundreds of years old, had been carefully carved out of the side of the cliff to enable the crossing of this harsh terrain at a reasonable and safe gradient. Paved with cobbles and stone steps, large sections of it still survive. It was a delight for walkers, but nowadays even several thousand hikers a year would not justify the building and maintenance of such a route. How was the cost justified in medieval times? The answer was salt. In the Middle Ages its importance and value justified the cost of building the track. The salt trade collapsed during the fifteenth century but those graded paths have survived as a monument to the engineering skills of our predecessors.

The route crossed the River Vesubie by a narrow, single-span arch, high above the water. I stood on the bridge and gazed down on the steel blue water gurgling through water-polished rocks the size of dinosaurs' eggs. With the recent dry weather the water lever was low, but even so there were bubbling white cascades and deep, pale blue pools amongst the rocks. I scrambled down a briary bank to the river bed, found a few bushes for the pretence of privacy, and within seconds I was gasping and splashing in the altogether. This was the third cold bath of the trip; I was becoming Spartan in my old age. The dip was so invigorating that I hardly noticed the hour's steep climb to Levens. The sound of young children happily playing in the School of St Roch indicated that he was still keeping his benevolent eye on things.

Although the church at Levens first entered the written record in 1286 and underwent restoration in 1614, it sits on very old foundations. Strange Romanesque heads decorate the feet of the columns, which lead to a claim that there was a pre-Christian temple on the site, a claim borne out by the carved Latin inscriptions built randomly into the walls of houses throughout the town. There are two attractive Baroque Chapels, both recently restored with simple elevations of stone quoins framing walls of pastel render. The Black Penitents, like their brothers in Briançon, have a very pretty, off-pink Chapel in which to conduct their dark business with the dead. The White Penitents have an equally cheerful, blue-rendered Chapel from which well-intentioned nobles and merchants conducted an early form of the welfare state by providing medical services for those unable to afford them.

December 8 was a special day in Levens. On that day in 1738, as an outbreak of plague threatened to spread up the valley, the townsfolk vowed *en masse* to the Virgin Mary that if she protected them they would always remember her. The plague by-passed the place and they were true to their promise.

The Grimaldis once owned Levens and in 1475 the family granted a Charter, no doubt for a hefty fee, allowing the townspeople to administer their own affairs. In spite of this, the family must have continued to interfere, because the townsfolk rose against them in 1621. But it was not until 1700 that Duke Victor Amadeus granted a further Charter by which the town of Levens became a 'Countess of Herself'. This is a fanciful way of saying that the Town Council had the privilege and authority of a Countess; presumably without any conjugal obligations to a Count.

Surely I have met Duke Victor Amadeus before? Almost; but not quite. From Samoens to Levens I had walked for three weeks, either through or close to the ancient and autonomous Duchy of Savoie. It was the seventh Duke Amadeus who planted that legendary lime tree to commemorate his Charter to Samoens in 1437. Allowing twenty-five years for each generation, the Duke Victor Amadeus who granted a charter to Levens would be his great-great-great-great-great-great-great-great-great grandson. Hereditary dukes need to be good at counting.

Again, I realised that my simple notion that France had always been France was wrong. At various times the Princes of Nice, the Kings of Sardinia and the Dukes of Savoie have ruled Levens. It was part of France during the Revolution but at the fall of Napoleon it reverted to Sardinia. The fair, but fickle, Countess of Levens did not become irrevocably French until as recently as 1860.

The Auberge de Mas Fleuri just outside Levens, came to meet me out of a typical Provençal watercolour; a picture of pastel colours and perfect, symmetrical proportions. The house had cream-rendered walls, white-painted windows and reveals, lilac-blue stained shutters, capped by a pantiled roof in faded pinks and creams. The garden was hardly formal and the owners' young children used most of it as a play area but there was enough foliage and flower-colour to frame and set off the house. I booked for the night, resisting the temptation to book for a week.

Dieter was a hairy man. The waves of billowing hair on his head were supported by forests of facial hair; the drooping moustache of a Viking warlord, the arched and shaggy eyebrows of a High Court Judge and hair sprouting untamed from his ears and nostrils. But most striking were his huge brown eyes that twinkled continuously and positively sparkled when he smiled. We introduced ourselves on the terrace and shared a table for dinner. He was walking for a few days in the Vesubie Valley and I tried not to be smug about my twenty-six days on the GR5. His conversation matched his appearance, flowing, extrovert and charming. He squeezed his whole life story into three courses. His father had left him a successful horticultural business at home in Germany, but his heart was not in it and he sold up. He was doing what he loved; making puppets and giving shows to children. Looking at him, how could I ever have imagined that he was on this earth for any other purpose?

The evening meal left me in no doubt as to where I was. The Provencal picture of the house was emphasised by the fixed-menu meal. It commenced with Tian of Courgettes Provencale, followed by a beef course called Daube Provencale, each well escorted on its way by AOC Blanc de Provence. Surely if I had parachuted blindfold on to that terrace from outer space, I would have known exactly where I was in the world by the time I got to the second course. Then came a surprise; camargue was a new cheese for me. It must be from Provence otherwise it would not have been on the premises; made with sheep's milk and rolled with herbs it was ideal to clear the palate between main courses. I finished with a locally-made (of course) Lemoncello liqueur and *café au lait*. Much to my surprise, Monsieur did not claim that he grew the coffee beans himself on some suitable Provençal slope. Even so, who would want to be parachuted anywhere else for dinner?

After a superb *prix fixe* meal, I lay in bed replete and satisfied, browsing through some tourist leaflets. Half asleep, I had a brainwave. There is a book I must write. Roughly titled 'Bloomers in Translation' it would include the best corkers that the French have produced in translating their promotional literature into English. For example, if I went canonying at Levens I could relax in the comforting knowledge that I would have the support of 'guides and experimental people'.

.P.R.'01

Chapter Twenty-Eight

Au Revoir, St Roch

The four small hill-towns of Roure, Utelle, Levens and Apremont have certain similarities. Their street plans resemble concentric corkscrews that get tighter and tighter towards the centre. The further south the villages, the less severe the terrain and the more spread out the general layouts. The four are like a set of Russian Dolls; each as pretty as the next and each one that much bigger. The houses, sometimes four storeys high, generally have no frontage, except in Apremont, the largest of the four, but even here goods-delivery must be a problem. Everything, from grand pianos to wardrobes must be carried from the bottom of the hill, through the gates and up to the house. The churches dominate each town from the rocky peak at the centre; it is not quite necessary to use ropes and crampons to get to Mass, but by the time I had climbed the steep slope to church on Sunday I could claim to have done my penance before I had made my confession.

Apremont was the largest, prettiest yet least interesting of all the hill-towns on the GR5. Unlike the other three, the tidal wave of international property price increases sweeping up from the coast has engulfed it. Every building was immaculate, every wall was freshly-painted. It did not feel real. Life is ups and downs; history is swings and roundabouts; buildings come and go. With all the buildings looking new, though I knew they must be old, it was like a toy village, and was discomforting.

The last hill on the journey was Mont Cime. To a walker who had climbed for four or five hours to gain mountain ridges for day after day after day it seemed a presumptuous name for a hill that took ten minutes to conquer. Appropriately enough I had a guard of honour to escort me up that last hill. A french partridge, its white throat distinguishing it from our more mundane grey partridge, ceremoniously progressed in front of me. She waddled a few paces, stopped, cast her head first to one side then to the other, waiting for me to catch up and then waddled on. She reminded me that I had left a grey partridge sitting on a nest of twenty or so eggs in my garden at home and I hoped that no harm had come to her. My french partridge led me the hundred yards to the top before flying off, presumably for ceremonial duties elsewhere.

There was not much to enjoy on the walk from Apremont to Nice other than the anticipation of the end of the journey. The path was stony, the rocks were hazardous, there were dry, ground-hugging plants, only a few flowers and thus even fewer butterflies. Finally there were a few hundred yards of descent through overgrown and neglected olive-groves. Today the olive is hardly worth the labour costs of its harvest A few, young brave souls are going back into olive production, hoping to find lucrative niche markets for specialised products. I wished them success. There is a long way to go before market trends will alter the gloomy funereal aspects of the last mile of the GR5 on what should be its triumphal entry into Nice. The route creeps in by the postern-gate when the city should welcome its long-distance Randonneurs with a ceremonial arcade of pines, if not with a handshake and gold medal from the Mayor.

I caught up with Dieter and he dissipated the gloom of the olive groves. We finished marching side by side singing together lustily 'Will you still need me, will you still feed me, when I'm sixty-four?' I suspect that was an irrelevant question for both of us but we made a fine pair; I knew the words and he knew the tune.

The first building we came to in Nice was a drive-in pharmacist. Suddenly, I was back in the twenty-first century with a bang! What on earth did the world want with a drive-in chemist's shop? I had been short of water purification tablets for a few days but I had in mind buying small bottle of about a hundred tablets and slipping them in my pocket. The idea of rolling up in a pick-up truck and bulk-buying a hundred years' supply had not entered my last-century brain. It is just possible that I am losing touch with the modern world.

The second building was neither funereal nor aggressively modern. It was my ideal Auberge, with a garden, and I could not pass it by. Dieter and I had a valedictory lunch amongst the flowers. Smiling waitresses immediately quenched my thirst with a bottle of mineral water from Evian les Bains, the very place on Lake Geneva where I had disembarked twenty-seven walking days ago. That small coincidence told me that the end of one journey is but the beginning of another. I should not be thinking of the ending of this trip, I should be planning the next. It is amazing what philosophical gems I can squeeze out of a small bottle of water!

Dieter walked off to catch his bus back to his puppet shows in Bavaria, leaving me outside the Auberge with a problem to consider. I was at a junction of six roads. That is not possible, my engineer's mind told me, so I sat back to watch. There were some rather faint road-markings to indicate priority, all of which seemed to be ignored by the average driver. I sat there for twenty minutes in mid-afternoon and there was not much traffic. Yet whenever two cars approached simultaneously there was almost an accident. Every encounter was accompanied by a lot of horn-blowing, tyre-screeching and the very last-minute application of brakes. Everybody got a little agitated, but nobody got angry. That is France for you; sometimes it should not work, but generally it does.

It would not happen in England. After months of surveys, road engineers would identify the two least-used roads. Bulldozers would demolish old stone walls, lorries would cart away tons of soil and bring in tons of tarmac until each of those two minor roads could form a T-junction with one of the remaining four roads many yards back. By the time they were done only four roads would meet at a neat central roundabout and the traffic would flow in an orderly fashion. If it did not, there might be a blast on the horn and a rude sign. That is England for you; generally it should work but sometimes it does not.

As far as the signposts are concerned, the GR5 finished there at the outskirts of Nice. There were no further signs to lead me downhill through the city to the beach. I did not want to trudge through suburbs anyway, so I caught the bus. The tourist literature on the bus informed me that the main hospital in Nice was the Hopital St Roch. In some form or another, whether it was a small shepherds' shrine in the hills, a chapel in the woods, a village school, or a city hospital, he had been with me all along my journey. Whether his presence had provided protection was a matter of faith. Certainly, I had come to no harm. I had suffered no cuts or bruises, no gyppy-tummy in twenty-seven days of walking, which was surprising, even if not certifiably miraculous.

Once I was in a town, I had urgent business to attend to. I found a Gents' Outfitter and remedied the problem that had been bugging me for twelve days. Then I reminded myself that I had walked through fabulous mountains for twenty-seven glorious days; travelling by bus to a modern shopping centre brought the walk to a finish with all the drama of a damp squib. That was not the way to end such an expedition. I decided to walk the last few yards from the bus-stop to the beach.

I finished as I had started; shoulders back, chest out, chin in, both arms swinging. Marching proudly in my dirty shorts and crumpled panama I might have been a teeny bit out of place. Chic Niceans, elegantly-dressed and perfumed, nudged and winked as

I passed. They were sophisticated people of the world, they knew what was going on. This was obviously a publicity-stunt for a remake of 'The Bridge over the River Kwai'. With Colonel Bogey ringing in my ears, I reached the shore and let the Mediterranean wash the dust from my sandals. My journey was complete.

I celebrated with a fine dinner in a quality restaurant overlooking the sea on the Promenade Anglais, which seemed aptly named for the occasion. Over the meal, I reviewed my days of walking. I thought contentedly of the clematis and the edelweiss, the trees, that ibex, the black woodpeckers. I could still see the impressive mountains, particularly my favourite; Mont Blanc. Then I remembered the abandoned defence works littered along that ancient border. Half of me was thankful that the fortifications had never been used in anger; the other half of me got annoyed at the evidence of huge, unnecessary defence expenditure. More politicians should walk the GR5.

My mind wandered back to previous trips into other mountains. I relived my initiation on Ben Nevis. After that first climb, I have been back over the years to tick off nearly all of the Scottish Munros and I have climbed and trekked in mountains in every continent of the world in the past twenty years. I recalled an attack of altitude sickness on Kilimanjaro, spine-tingling fears of heights on Kinabalu, bottled drinking water frozen solid on Mont Blanc and revolting porters on Cotopaxi. As the meniscus in my wine bottle dropped, I became mellower as I thought of treks in the Himalayas, in the Atlas and in New Zealand. I had enjoyed them all. There is a debate on the Internet, mainly among Americans, as to which is the finest Grand Route in the World – is it the GR5 or the Anapurna Circuit? Both routes are outstanding treks in so many different ways that there is absolutely no sense in trying to rank them. Do them both and stop arguing. Every trip I have made has given me something different and something special. And so my thoughts came round full-circle to the GR5. Certainly it had given me days of delight walking through beautiful scenery, an abundance of colourful flora and interesting fauna, attractive villages and people who were mostly friendly and helpful. With the wine dregs I began to think of my next trip. There would have to be mountains, of course, but preferably with managed Refuges remote in the wilderness. There should be villages every third or fourth day with comfortable inns serving good food and decent wines. There must be well-protected environments rich in flowers, insects, birds and mammals. Finally, there had to be warm, outgoing and friendly people. I expect next year I will be walking in my own way in France.

I booked into Nice Airport very early for my flight and looked for a chapel. In medieval times most international travellers were faithful pilgrims, with chapels and shrines dominating their routes. In this age of cheap flights, international travellers are more likely to be pleasure-seekers, duty-free shops marking their routes. The huge complex of international aviation at Nice is a masterpiece of the application of reason to function; but that leaves precious little room for faith. The small chapel was an afterthought, and I eventually found it tucked away in a corner. I knelt for a few minutes in appreciative solitude before leaving on the altar rail an envelope addressed to St Roch. Inside were some Euro notes and two small silver-foil packets, unopened. The priest who finds it will probably frown in puzzlement, but the recipient will smile in complete understanding.

I boarded my plane and flew back to the Age of Reason.